When the Universe Speaks

Nina Russo

Copyright © 2019 Nina Russo

All rights reserved.

ISBN: 978-1-0705-6049-6

FOREWORD

The most well-rounded people I have ever met have gone through some shit. Trauma sucks. It breaks you down, suffocates you, and robs you of so many things. However— **if** you persevere, **if** you somehow can conjure up resilience— your trauma just may be the thing that transforms you.

When I first met Nina, I felt connected instantly. Light workers recognize Light workers, and often what is unspoken is still understood. I felt her light and, consequently, I felt her pain. It wasn't the kind of pain that was crippling to her presently, but it was there— dormant under her flawless exterior. Most people don't welcome pain. I used to run from it, avoid it, search for a way around it. If there was a potential to get hurt, I made a U-turn. Back then, I wasn't aware that pain and trauma could lead me to freedom. I had zero inclination that the hardest moments of my life would lead me to the greatest version of myself. How could I have known? Nina didn't know either. I'm not sure any of us ever do.

In the beginning of 2019, I lost a child to a miscarriage. I fell deeply into my third bout of postpartum depression and I nearly died. I spent weeks in bed (both my own and the beds in the University of North Carolina Women's Center for Perinatal Mood Disorders). In our toughest moments, we forget. We forget that we have always made it through our toughest moment. We forget what we are capable of. We forget who we are. In my toughest moment, lying in bed, I forgot. Nina's words— her story — leapt off the page and helped me remember. They spoke to me. Her resounding words reminded me that, although I had experienced something awful, if I could hold on and push through, I may just come out of it not just as a survivor, but thriving.

If you have ever gone through a spiritual awakening, you recognize the symptoms in others. It's hard to describe the freedom felt from awakening to a person who has yet to awaken, but you want it for them and you wish it for them. As I read *When the Universe Speaks*, I knew, without a doubt, that Nina had experienced an awakening. The power, light and beauty in her words made it evident. For years I spoke to God/Universe and heard nothing. Maybe I wasn't ready. Maybe it wasn't my time to become one with the Universe. Maybe that is only possible to do when you see God and/or the Universe in yourself. When you realize that you ARE the Universe and that we all are. I see God in everything now. Flowers are more beautiful, I hear music differently, and I am completely grounded for the first time in my life. I didn't get here on my own. It was a complex journey. What it really comes down to is something that both Nina and I know with every fiber of our beings: When the Universe Speaks… LISTEN! It will change your life. Believe me, it saved mine.

Danni Starr

Author:

Empathy and Eyebrows A Survivalist's Stories on Reviving Your Spirit After Soul-Crushing Sh*tstorms

AUTHOR'S NOTE

This book began as a personal release of the experiences that launched my holistic growth— mind, body, and spirit. Although this book has grown with me over the past two years, self-discovery begins but doesn't really ever end. I decided to share this journey of my encounters with the people and circumstances that brought me to this very moment and space in my life. For me, it was through the lessons and blessings with these people and places that propelled me into alignment with my highest purpose. At the root of each experience was a guiding energy. It was only when I ignored the signs that I found myself imbalanced and lost. By sharing myself, as just an average, every-day woman, my sole desire is to penetrate the soul of the girl or woman reading this and have her gasp with relief— "I'm not alone in this." And then, fill her with *hope*— a knowing that she is valid and unstoppable.

As unique as we are, we are just as much the same,

and I want us to connect through our experiences, turmoil, emotions, and ultimately, our triumphs. Far and wide, we are a tribe. We are a phenomenon. To every girl or woman who has ever felt less than. To every girl or woman who has ever felt silenced. To every girl who has never lived in self-truth. To every girl who has never discovered self-worth. To every girl who has had her shine dimmed. That was me before emerging from the rubble. So firstly, I wrote this for me. But I know that sharing can break barriers; that vulnerability can counteract isolation.

Taylor Swift once leaned in to her microphone at her concert, with a devilish look on her face, and said, "If you don't want songs written about you, then don't do bad things." Mic drop. Epic. While I do share the raw, uncut stories about people and experiences, the intention is never to bash, but instead only to use these situations as a vehicle to grow and flourish.

Lastly, there is a theme throughout the book involving the partnership between the Universe and self. Honoring our intuition and inner being boosts our connectedness with the Universe. Self-empowerment and self-healing take a front seat. But there is something I must address when it comes to the well-being of our mind, body, and spirit, and that is mental health. Sometimes our bodies physically get sick. We catch a common cold or other illness and have to take the necessary steps to get our health back on track. If our physical bodies get sick, wouldn't it make sense that our mental wellness may fluctuate, too? Much like a common cold that we can remedy at home, sometimes our brain chemistry is off and we can get it back to optimal health on our own or through other simple means. But what happens when that cold gets more serious? When it turns into pneumonia or a chronic lung illness? We absolutely need medical and professional intervention. The same goes for mental decline. We can't self-sooth all the time. Taking care of our mental is just as vital as attending to our physical health because holistic health is not one or the other— it's the unified well-being of the mind, body and spirit.

Washington, D.C.

DEAR UNIVERSE

You and I weren't always so connected. I remember going about my day thinking your powers were way up in the sky. I said my prayers and believed in karma. I went to Catholic schools and was introduced to a version of you that felt a bit limited. You were present, but distant. I would see other people with a much closer relationship with you, and I always wondered exactly how that came to be. Those people seemed to be so happy, positive, and grounded all the time. I wanted that!

We finally met through a sort of forced connection. Certain events unfolded and I realized that the only way out of these situations wasn't by looking up at you, but by going through you. Once I started to really get in tune with you, my perspective shifted and my spirits were uplifted. I couldn't "unsee" your magic. I went on a venture of self-study to keep uncovering the depths of your beauty and abundance. I started to get specific when I spoke to you, and that's when things really started to propel forward at lightning speed. I began to recognize that every major obstacle was the precursor for deepening the connection. I finally understood that all those people who saw your light, first had to see their own darkness.

The previously distant presence of yours turned into a very close and intimate connectedness. We weren't lightyears apart, but instead we intertwined and co-existed. Those of us who have awakened to your light have had very different ways of reaching that point. The beauty is that even with various means of getting there, becoming deeply connected to you also connected us with each other. We have a soul-felt understanding with one another. Those of us who have come out of the trenches know that it doesn't matter how grave or minor the circumstances were leading up to the uncovering of your Universal powers. Once we know the light, we become the light.

Through becoming more connected to you, we have in turn become more connected to our own inner truth. We have learned to operate from the heartfelt space, to overcome limiting beliefs, and to trust in your infinite guidance. Perhaps the best revelation of all is that looking within ourselves is essentially looking into the Universe—the answers aren't far and wide, but instead are divinely tucked inside of us.

THE POWER OF THREE

"Your values create your internal compass that can navigate how you make decisions in your life. If you compromise your core values, you go nowhere."

Roy T. Bennett

You never quite understand the impact family life has on the framing of your character until you wake up one day with an *ah ha!* moment and are able to pinpoint your upbringing as the source of your expectations. Expectations for life matters— friendships, dating, work. Growth has a way of taking you back to these molding roots. For me, the realization came about during the year after graduating from college. Until that point, I had been living life true to my convictions, but clueless as to where these truths derived from. *I do not understand how someone can be like this* was nearly a daily thought across several interactions.

I grew up in a very tight-knit family. My grandparents were married at 19, my parents married each other at 22. Early adulthood family building is ingrained in our family dynamic. I did not have home life issues, my parents rarely fought, we didn't struggle financially... this was my normal, the basis for which I believed the average family to operate. It was (and has always been) family first— no matter what. I envisioned my adulthood to follow this "normal." Get married young, keep the Italian culture alive, work a 9-5, buy a house, have children, and stay close to the family proximity wise. I knew nothing else. Before going further, this is not meant to elicit a, "Poor her— having a normal life yet seeking pity" sentiment. It is my pure intention to encourage reflection on time periods and events that have such a shaping effect on who we are. Throughout this book, you will see that while the trajectory of what my "normal" life would look like drastically took some twists and turns, some of these *core* values remained constant.

Although my entire family deserves recognition, especially my mom and sister who will get their time to shine later in the book, being a young adult woman has had me deeply reflect on the three greatest examples of selflessness and decency. They say that a woman subconsciously seeks a partner with similar qualities to those of her father. So that's where I'll start; sharing with you the greatest man I'll ever know.

My dad and I are complete opposites. He is calm, patient, quiet, somber, and I... well, you get the picture. He has always exhibited the utmost selfless behavior. From my disastrous behavior as a child, to my outspoken ways as an adult, he has remained constant in his nature. My mom, sister, and I can rely on him for anything and everything. He anticipates our needs before we even ask. There is literally NOTHING he wouldn't do for us. So, again, this was my normal! A selfless, loving farther figure is a representation of how all men will treat me, right?! Don't worry— I'm laughing at my naivety, too.

The apple must not have fallen far from the tree, because the next attribution of pure love is my grandfather, my dad's dad. May he rest in peace with my grandma, that man was a silent beacon of giving. The man rarely ever spoke, but the love for his family was heard at the highest of volumes through his actions. He lived in Sicily, and when we'd visit, he'd so generously slip my sister and me $50 for some "gelato." Everyday. For three weeks. My admiration for him grew even more towards the end of his life. My grandmother had been in poor health for a while. We all knew that her health was continuing to decline. My grandfather cared for her as best he could, along with my aunt and the in-home care. She came first. So much so, that he neglected to tell anyone of his own declining health as to not take away from the focus being on my grandmother. As a shock to us all, he had cancer and passed away before my grandmother. No one knew until the very end— the epitome of selflessness.

My mom's dad is right up here with these two. He moved to the United States in 1958, eventually brought my grandmother and their baby, and lived out the American dream. At 81 years old, he is still running his business that he built from the ground up all those years back. He is the jack-of-all-grandfathers. Need an electrician? He's there. Your roof needs repaired? He's on it. Literally. Your car broke down? Oh, you can borrow his. Giving is so second-nature to him. It's truly amazing to see. Never mention that you like the cookies he bought from Costco, unless you want basically a lifetime supply brought to you the following day. It's who he is. And when it comes to my grandma, he is her number one caretaker, shopping partner, and supporter. Ride or die.

I think by now you can see the intersectionality of normal and expectations. All I've known has been selflessness and reliability. Not just from these three men, but from the women in my family, as well. When it comes to dating and friendships, I quickly learned that my normal was just that, *my* normal. My expectations of reciprocated consideration were shut down on many occasions. At first, I was thoroughly confused as to why someone wouldn't exhibit these loving behaviors. Should I take it personally? If I had treated others with the same care that I witnessed my whole life, why can't they recognize and reciprocate? And then it dawned on me. It's not about me at all. We are all living products of our normal. Someone who never had a parental figure to rely on unconditionally, may not know how to exhibit that characteristic to anyone else. Now, of course, there are so many people who grow up in a toxic environment and decide to rise from the ashes. They vow to create a normal for themselves based on what they *didn't* have. But for others, recognizing the need to alter, or break the cycle, is not as feasible. So, what do we do with the notion of not faulting anyone for their normal, but simultaneously holding them accountable for understanding right and wrong as an adult? I thought that maybe I would just have to find someone who shares the same "normal" as me. The truth is, we do not need to look for a mirrored normal. We need to look for the responses to it. This is why self-reflection is such an integral part of the growth process. Our values, beliefs, and convictions have all stemmed from our exposure. As adults, we have a responsibility to align ourselves correctly, as we are not only examples for generations below, but also as an obligation to our peers.

My normal may be damaging to my expectations. I noticed that in the past my standards had substantially lowered on the decency totem pole due to being repeatedly let down. I would catch myself pondering if my expectations are just non-existent. Has the "ride or die" family sentiment diminished? Is it a generational flaw? I like my normal. It is comforting and secure. I would not be staying true to myself if I allowed the actions, or lack of actions of others, inhibit my desire to recreate this normal for my future family. And that has been the most beautiful lesson of all! It is easy to lose sight of long-held core values when exposed to people who do not share the same ones. Losing yourself before you've even found yourself is all too common. Our truth is designed for us. We can ignore it or try to make changes, but by doing so, we bring about a feeling of unfulfillment upon ourselves. No one else will hold us accountable to live out these truths. As humans, we are worthy of staying true to who we are and what we want. Find your power of three, your driving force behind the essence of your core, and be mindful about the duty you have to be the gatekeeper in preserving your values and your truth.

New York, New York

SICILY

"There are only two lasting bequests we can give our children— one is roots, and the other, wings."

Hodding S. Carter

Summer 2016 was one of the greatest markers in my journey of self and spiritual growth. As a college graduation gift from my parents, I went to Sicily for two weeks with my aunt and her family. Our entire family history is on this island. I had been to Sicily before, but never without my immediate family. I was slightly nervous, but extremely excited nonetheless. Little did I know, these next two weeks would be the propeller of an inner shift in my adulthood. The rattling before the earthquake, per se. Early mornings on the beach, late nights partying, it was easily the best vacation I had been on yet. In the midst of soaking in the Mediterranean sun and embracing the night life, I felt at home. My father was born and raised in this town in Sicily, and my mother's family was also from the same little town. Ironically, my parents met there while my mom was on vacation one summer. A feeling washed over me and I realized more than ever that I wanted to really get deeply in touch with my cultural roots. The desire for my idea of "normal" was resurfacing.

    I came home after the trip feeling utterly confused, but tremendously certain at the same time. I had to end a relationship that no longer served me or the other person, struggling to make a decision that two weeks prior was not high on my radar. After the breakup, I found myself in contact with someone who I had met in Sicily, realizing the potential to follow in the footsteps of my parents. I belonged in Sicily. The European lifestyle had always appealed to me. Months went by before the post vacation blues had subsided. I contemplated moving to Italy and teaching English. As much as I wanted to do it, there was a part of me that was hesitant to make such a drastic move on my own. The idea slowly vanished from my mental focus, but buried itself deep within as a burning desire.

    That trip really ignited a shift in me. It brought me back to my roots and forced me to reassess the way I had been letting life lead me, instead of the other way around. It truly did uncover the layers I had unknowingly been stacking on top of my familial origins. I went to Sicily for a fun summer vacation, never expecting that sense of connection to the land of my ancestors to take such firm hold of me. It was a really confusing identity battle, to say the least. On the one hand, I felt pulled in the direction of completely boxing myself in the culture. On the other, I had lifestyle desires and goals that didn't quite align with the full cultural immersion. As much as I adore Sicily and its traditions, it is not rich or fertile in the "sky is the limit" approach to life. It wasn't until later down the road did I realize that I didn't have to choose between where I came from and where I wanted to go— that my roots and my wings could absolutely share the same space. I could remain grounded in heritage *and* take flight in personal growth. I feel blessed to be able to embrace both! This clarity wasn't always there, though. The sort of tug-of-war experience forced me to see that neglecting part of an identity in favor of another creates an emptiness. It truly was step one on the path of coming into my own.

I have learned so much from that point up until now, but one of the greatest lessons has been that every single thing happens when it is supposed to and for a specific reason. Divine timing is everything; what happens to you happens for you; and a shake-up is *always* a wake up.

Rome, Italy

THE EARTHQUAKE

"Emotions can get in the way or get you on the way."

Mavis Mazhura

I'm a sucker for viewing the unexpected as divine gifts from the Universe. I gasp with that open mouth grin thinking, "Wow, Universe, you really shouldn't have!" Sometimes, though, these gifts can come in the form of catalysts for personal and spiritual growth. Out of nowhere, I met someone who I instantly clicked with, and who also clicked with my family. We'll call him Chris. The connection was fire. The relationship escalated quickly, flowed effortlessly, and truly seemed too good to be true. And that's because it was. Love bombing at its finest. The relationship only lasted a couple of months, ending as quickly as it started. I was *ugly* devastated.

It was the first time that I understood how meaningless the construct of time is. I spent years with people and wasn't nearly as torn as I was after those couple short months. I was at my lowest point, swarmed in a mess of emotions. I was left suddenly and left without answers. I couldn't get through a single day without breaking down. It was my first actual heartbreak, and it was rough. As awful as it was, it was one of the most beautiful gifts life could have given me. I realized my strength and resilience. I turned to self-help books that put me on the path of growth that I would have never discovered had I not been crushed. I became much more in tune with the power of the Universe and understanding that there is always a greater purpose. The crippling sadness somehow re-sparked my creativity for writing and my drive to work towards a new career path in education. I realize now that I was too comfortable with the day-to-day life. I needed something to shake me to the core; almost as if a physical and emotional realignment occurred.

At the time, I had no idea how to cope with things like this. I was left to my own devices, but these devices were solely driven by emotion and the longing to need to know *why*. Trust me when I say that breakups can be the best things to ever happen to us. At the time, I would've described it as the most horrific and suffocating feeling. I wasn't aware that when people walk out, the Universe is creating space for something better. I wish I had known to let go in peace, and allow the grief to flow through me. I didn't know that emotional strength could not truly be possessed without an emotional trauma. I like to think of it in terms of training for a marathon. Most of us do not have the capability to get up one day to run a marathon without any preparation. It takes months of grueling practice in building stamina and endurance. It's not pretty, but without it, reaching the finish line would not be a possibility. Of course, trauma does not always have to be the precursor for beauty and growth, but it most definitely offers an invaluable shift in perspective We can find solace in knowing that heartbreaks are actually a blessing— our most vital muscle and organ becomes stronger. One thing that I know for certain is that even if given the opportunity to go back in time and avoid this experience, I absolutely would not. To anyone reading this who is facing a similar situation: cry, lay in bed, scream into your pillow, and then get up. You WILL get through it, and you will come out of it as a much better person. It is not to say that future disappointments will not have an impact on you, it is just that when they inevitably occur, you will know that there is light at the end. You will have a deeper connection with your ability to persevere and see through the unfortunate circumstance, and you will undoubtedly know the power of your own resilience.

Rome, Italy

ENERGY

"Never allow your ego to diminish your ability to listen."

Gary Hopkins

Self-discovery was on the rise after that shattering breakup. I was certain that I wouldn't let any red flags slip by again; any subsequent emotional wrecks could not possibly be as hard as that one. Nevertheless, the Universe had more lessons in store. 2017 was a year of finding myself through other people. Once I emerged out of the dark cave of feeling sorry for myself, I felt empowered, unstoppable. Out of nowhere, a good-looking guy approached me at the gym. The gym had been my safe haven, lifting (pun may be intended) my spirits after my roughest days. We exchanged numbers. I remember telling myself to keep reserved in order to avoid another rushed relationship that could potentially end terribly. I was open from day one about wanting to take my time getting to know him, and he completely understood. They say first impressions last a lifetime, but what they don't always emphasize is that even the *good* first impressions can have a particularly lasting effect.

    Damien had been doing everything right. It gave me great hope of being open to that connection again. He was inquisitive, communicative, and present. I felt secure in getting to know him. Until one day, everything changed. He became less responsive, less interested in meaningful conversation, less dependable. I was confused. What happened to the super friendly guy I met on the stair climber? I brought up my concerns and simply asked that he just be honest with his intentions. He attributed his recent disconnect to his demanding job and being in the process of purchasing a home. My empathetic nature can be too understanding at times; creating excuses rather than processing situations at face value. I felt as if I chose my battles wisely, and therefore, was completely stunned by the few times I would address these issues to him and be completely shut down or ignored. Maybe we just operate differently, I thought. I found myself in a constant downward spiral of negative energy. I would wake up in the morning and just be consumed with the feeling of "something is not right." The problem was that I didn't know what that "something" was. In my alone time, I'd fall into dark moments with my body telling me from the inside out that this was not normal. I should not be feeling this way. Whatever it was, I felt it in my core. I *heard* the energy, but I wasn't *listening* to it.

    The Universe can only whisper to you for so long

before the hints get louder. It had been a particularly rough few weeks. I was in a constant state of sadness, feeling like I was being put on the backburner. My energy had been depleted. My family and coworkers noticed that I was just going through the motions— lacking any spark or motivation. I was at my lowest once again.

    I had a trip to Greece coming up with my two best friends. I thought it would be the perfect time to recharge and come back refreshed. The Universe thought so, too. Two days before leaving for this highly anticipated vacation, the truth came to light. I had not been the only woman being entertained by Damien. After asking many times, after being led to believe that we were in an exclusive situation, my energy had been affirmed. It was a moment of disbelief *and* confirmation. Damien had asked me to think about what I wanted on the trip and discuss it together when I returned. I told him that I would consider, but truly did not see how I could ever trust him again.

    Picture this: the movie airport scene where two jaded lovers come to their senses and make that dramatic last-minute reconnection. And now picture the complete opposite of that. As my ride to the airport pulled up to my house, which happened to be my best friend's sweet grandparents in their minivan, he called me to disclose that "we should be friends because [I am] not looking for a relationship." Doorbell and phone rang at the exact same time; what a lovely combination! The anger instantly ignited. I had asked him many times if this was what he wanted, and even offered to remove myself without any drama. But he waited until an ugly truth was revealed and then suggested that we be friends? I tried my best not to allow this hurt to consume me in Greece. And I did a damn good job. I had the most amazing week of my life. The timing was perfect, and I am beyond grateful to the Universe for sending me a shock followed by comfort and serenity. I do not believe in coincidences.

For the first time in a long time, I wasn't trying to force or understand where I stood with him. I was hurt. And I allowed myself to actually feel the hurt, instead of trying to mask it or reach out to him. One of the hardest lessons I have come by is that *the source of hurt cannot be the source of healing.* Too many times, after being hurt by him or a previous person, I would vent to them about how they made me feel. I wanted them to understand the consequences of their actions, and ultimately hear the apologies as a form of validation that I had been successful in making them understand. If I had not been in Greece, maybe I would have fallen into the trap of continuing to express how wrong what he did was. Once I was back, I was vibrating so high. While still hurt, I had this new layer of skin. I was thoroughly content and enjoying life. I would ask the Universe just to give me a sign that he learned a lesson. I promised myself not to seek it out, but to just one day be able to know if he understood that his actions have a real and true impact on others. The day came. I saw him and received an unexpected apology. This is not to condone holding on to anger and hurt until we receive an apology. Most times, apologies never come but forgiveness is still necessary. I went through the hurt on my own, and this time, instead of me wanting him to feel sorry for me, I wanted him to learn a valuable life lesson for his own well-being. Spiritual growth has a way of shifting one's intentions and focus in light of adversity. My younger self would have hoped for something bad to happen to him, or for him to feel sorry for me and want me back. This time was different. It's not always about me. Sometimes my absence can be the channel for another person's growth; and that's okay, too.

Tuscany, Italy

CHECK YOUR CHAKRAS

"Take care of your body. It's the only place you have to live."

Jim Rohn

Once I returned home from Greece, I had an appointment that I made previously with an intuitive healer to have my chakras aligned. The first time I heard about chakras was over a year prior, soon after the terrible breakup with Chris. Around that time, a family friend of mine, Carmela, had asked me to attend an "Abundant Life Seminar" with her. I was expecting to be in an audience listening to a motivational speaker. This day has a particular significance. It had been exactly one month after "the" breakup with Chris, and I still found myself so confused. Why did he suddenly leave? He told me that he missed his ex-girlfriend, and that our "honeymoon stage" was over. My jaw dropped because he had only ever said negative things about the previous relationship. A month had passed, and I needed to know the truth. I knew deep down that there was more to the sudden change. I decided that I would wait a few more days, and then I was going to some way attempt reaching out to him. (The present day me would not do this now, by the way. If they leave, let them!) Well, on the day of the seminar, while at work, I was scrolling through Twitter. One mutual follower and a few clicks away, and the answer was finally revealed to me. He was back together with his ex and moved across the country to be with her.

    I was shattered once again, but I also finally had that closure. My emotions were incredibly high that day. I held myself together at work and almost decided not to go to the seminar. I went anyways, and am forever grateful that I did. This was yet another marker on the path of growth that I was on. Evolution happens in layers, and it's amazing to look back and see the significance of certain events. The seminar was actually a very intimate setting. There were six women, plus the life coach who led the session. We discussed the meaning of an abundant life, self-love, and participated in activities to bring forth abundance through creativity. Each of us spoke on what we like and dislike about ourselves, and I was a straight mess. I could not hold my tears back. The tears were definitely from sadness, but also from the utmost gratitude of this seminar being right on time.

    We eventually got on the topic of chakras and spiritual alignment. It was completely new for me. I researched it a bit after the session, and then sort of kept it in the back of my mind. Flash forward to the height of my energy being drained from the confusing situation I was in with Damien. My friend casually mentioned that she had seen an intuitive healer to have her chakras aligned. A lightbulb went off. I had to go. I immediately contacted Carmela and we decided that we would find time to go. Life took its course once again, and two months later, we finally made the appointment. I would be going two days after returning from Greece. Divine intervention, perhaps? I went to the appointment with zero expectations. I still did not really have a comprehensive understanding of what the session would entail, but I decided that I wanted to gain the fullest from it and not go in with any preconceived notions.

 I stepped into the room. The ambiance was relaxing with dim lighting, soothing music, and natural aromas. Immediately, the intuitive healer sensed that I had recently been spiraling into a depressive state, with lots of crying and uncertainty. She told me that I was recently in a situation where I was severely undervalued, that I had been deceived, and that I was on a new career path. This woman only knew my name. My first name, at that. I bawled my eyes out. There is something truly freeing in having such energy interpreted so accurately. It not only affirmed my feelings, but offered me a way to free myself of the toxicity. It was a moment that I will never forget as long as I live. Energy alignment is as much a priority as any other health check for me. The session was over, but it was time to put the tools she provided me with to use. She explained to me that I had a huge difficulty communicating with myself—battling if my feelings stem from intuition or past experiences. In strengthening the intuitive muscle, it was imperative that I listen to my guides even in the most minor of circumstances. Additionally, she told me that I absolutely needed to use forgiveness as the mechanism for releasing pain. Sigh. I took a deep breath. My energy was realigned, but if I was not careful and didn't put in the inner work *after* the session, I could easily fall back into that whirlwind of darkness and tangled up energy.

    I cannot stress enough how emotional health is just as important as physical health. If we don't actively keep our energy in check, it creates a domino effect. Mental health starts to dwindle, physically we do not feel our best, and emotionally we become totally imbalanced. We seek medical attention or use home remedies when we have a sore throat. We have to keep this same proactive approach to our overall well-being. Self-care is a great preventative tool, but sometimes those shocks come in and throw us way out of whack. Energetic blocks or emotional imbalances not only significantly impact our lives, but they inevitably bleed onto all other aspects of life, such as friendships, relationships, and work. We have strayed away from these ancient healing practices so much so that most people (especially in the Western world) are not even aware that energy healing is vital to overall health. Let's make checking our chakras and healing our energy just as mainstream as any other physical check-ups! Chakra challenge, anyone?

Rome, Italy

INDIFFERENCE

"The opposite of love is not hate, it's indifference."

Elie Wiesel

When it comes to relationships, hate would not exist without some form of passionate attachment. I learned this one the hard way. As Chris spoke so terribly about his previous relationship, he elevated me on a pedestal in comparison to the trauma and toxicity she brought to his life. He could have equally had a part in their toxic relationship, but the focus here is recognizing this hatred as a continued hurt, rather than a healed trauma. I started to look at how I viewed and talked about past relationships. I remember after one messy relationship, all I had to say about this person were nasty, negative things. And rightfully so! But it wasn't until one day, the thought or mention of him did not serve as a trigger. Anger and hurt did not flare up; I had a neutral feeling about him. Indifference— fully healed and fully let go. The same can be said about Damien. I had this deep seeded anger built up towards him and tried to conceptualize his behavior. I would say things about him that, although were coming from the perspective of my truth about the experience with him, were negative and the complete opposite of indifference. The energetic grip was still present. Now, I am able to share my truth without the troubled energetic reaction attached to it.

Pay attention to how someone speaks about previous relationships. If it's harsh and negative, run. There is a difference between someone being able to objectively share their past experience versus sharing the past experience with an escalated emotional attachment. This person may not be aware that this hatred is indicative of an incomplete healing process. And please do not begin another relationship until you have hit the indifference phase. When you dislike someone to the core, you believe you are over them, right? Wrong. You're hurt. Someone you do not love or care about cannot cause you to harbor ill feelings. Allow yourself the time to process the situation and put in the work to heal. After a while, remaining hurt becomes a choice. Yes, there is an appropriate grieving process. It takes time for the heart to filter through the emotions and release the past pain. But at a certain point, you choose to remain in the dark, or you choose to create the light. Shed the cloak of hate, and open yourself to be wrapped in armor of love. Be grateful that you are no longer associated with someone who had the power to strip you of your peace. Embrace the endless possibilities of the future. But please do not entrap an innocent person into a field of chaos. It creates a tremendous mix of energy. It is unfair to allow the blood of past wounds to drip on the present, and it is equally unfair to expect someone else to patch up these wounds. Get to that point of indifference, wish the past well, and *then* share your magic with someone else.

LOST AND FOUND

"Make sure you are responding to the present moment and not reacting to something from your past the current situation reminds you of."

Maryam Hasnaa

I used to live with this notion of having lost myself before I had even found myself. Only through the coldest rejection with Chris was I able to discover myself on the deepest and most intimate level. It was everything I needed and more. The scary part, though, was losing myself again— my newly discovered, deeply connected self. I cannot put the entire blame on Damien. He showed me who he was. I didn't believe it because I was so focused on the initial showing of himself. I don't know why the 180 occurred, but what I do know is that *when people show you who they are, believe them*. And believe them the first time! After the first shift and switch up, I was confused. But the shift and switch up continued. My energy was physically warning me.

As humans, we have ruined our intuitive abilities with rationality. Although intuition is largely connected to our evolution, our evolution as rational beings has been our greatest strength, and equally our greatest downfall. I have been able to push through the emotionally confusing experiences only by looking for the lesson. Answers, clarity, and honesty will not always be present. Sometimes our most reliable source of understanding comes directly from our intuition, our vibes, our energy. Becoming less reliant on rationality and communication from others is something that I work on relentlessly. It is incredibly difficult to basically not use your brain and rely solely on the "gut feeling." The more you listen, the stronger it becomes, until it is just second nature. I like to think of it as a "use it or lose it" situation.

I know that this idea begs the question: *What if you're just assuming, your perceived intuition is completely wrong, or you misinterpret the entire situation?* Part of my struggle with Damien was this idea that I was misinterpreting my gray and gloomy feelings. So, I adapted and discovered a new way to navigate. I address the gut feeling. Is it organic? Am I assuming or comparing the current situation to a previous one? Am I in a low emotional state, where everything could be interpreted through the lens of this negativity? Am I particularly anxious about something? It's really important to be able to decipher between a perceived and actual intuitive response. It took me a while, but after trial and error, the answer revealed itself to me. It is simply being able to differentiate between the *feeling* and the *thought*.

Intuition manifests itself as the all-encompassing feeling in our body, typically felt most in the abdomen region, hence the "gut feeling." Sometimes it is a random flash of a thought that you did not actively create. Embrace this *knowing*. Intrusive thoughts are just that— thoughts. They stem from scenarios we conjure up in our minds. The thoughts are directly tied to our previous programming. If we've been in threatening situations before, we carry this subconscious response with us and end up projecting past hurts onto present experiences. The programming really does have a way of altering our perception of reality to match that of a familiar pattern of the past.

My friends once asked me how to know the difference between their intuition and anxious projection. In the most simplistic of ways— intuition is a feeling first and a thought second, whereas projection is a thought first and a feeling second. Intuition happens in the present moment; projection is based on past exposure. It can be incredibly confusing to decipher between the two. Sit in silence. Inhale and exhale. Focus solely on the breathing. Once the body is relaxed and calm, you will know. And once you know, *trust* it. Once the body knows, allow the mind to follow suit. I want to note that this may not apply to those who suffer from anxiety regularly. I am only referring to individuals who may have anxious thoughts about certain situations, but do not suffer from a diagnosed anxiety disorder.

In order to continue to strengthen my ability to listen to my intuition, I have tried to hold myself accountable by following through with even the most minute "gut feelings" I have. For instance, going through one doorway instead of another because "something" is steering me in that direction; I have made it a point to listen and follow.

Although I am aware that I lost myself before I found myself, and subsequently lost myself so soon after, I had to put in the necessary work to ensure that it never happens again. I owe that to myself. Losing my shine, my worth, and my self-value was a terrifying experience. I look back and see how it slowly but surely unfolded. Will I recognize this spiral if I happen to be in a similar situation in the future? I sure hope so. But only I can hold myself fully accountable. As soon as we feel that we are veering away from our authenticity, or not being valued, we have to remove ourselves with grace— quickly and affirmatively.

Once you remove yourself, don't question it. Thoughts of doubt will creep in making you believe that you have made the wrong decision. When we're in a situation that we w*ant* to be in, but know we *should not* be in, there is a battle between the heart and mind. Interestingly, we feel it in our hearts first. We have been told that "the heart has trouble accepting what the mind knows." Upon really reflecting on how things transpire, it's actually the complete opposite. The mind takes longer to catch up. Think of it in the opposite scenario. You've met someone that you are really feeling a connection with. Time goes on, feelings become stronger, and eventually there is a flutter in the heart. You're in love! Your heart knows it. Your mind however— "What if it's too soon to say it?!" "Is this really love?" "Is it weird to express it?" "What if he doesn't say it back?"

Hello! Do you see what I'm saying?! We feel it first, and think it second. The mind lags behind. After we let go of what is no longer serving us, the energy from the situation is still flowing through us, manifesting as thought. We want nothing more than to "fix" this seemingly wrong situation. We're fooled into thinking that going back in time will offer the emotional comfort and protection that is so desperately desired after leaving something or someone behind. Allow the thoughts to flow through without analyzing them. Blocking the organic movement of these thoughts by layering them with deep analysis creates a long, drawn out detour for that energy to be released. I know that it's hard to avoid dissecting these thoughts and to avoid assigning emotional responses to them, but I also know that it's possible. Mind, body, and soul operate as one. When there is a misalignment, that's when we continue to suffer in emotional distress. You have this innate power and the control to feel more and think less. Will you use it?

Rome, Italy

ILLUSION OF POTENTIAL

"Don't blame a clown for acting the clown, ask yourself why you keep going to the circus."

Unknown

One of the hardest pills to swallow is recognizing and accepting the illusion of potential. How many times have you stayed with someone, not because of what *is,* but because of what *could be?* It's a heavy concept to sift through. You see this potential greatness. You get taste tests of it here and there, but the full course meal has not yet been served. Think of it this way— you just started going to a new hair stylist. She did a really great job with the simple cut you asked of her the first time you went. The next couple times were also good, but you're ready to take it to the next level and get yourself a new do. She attempts your vision, but falls short of really capturing your idea and transforming your current style. You give her another chance because you saw a really great color job she did to a client once on her Instagram. You know she has it in her to give you this trendy, chic look you're dying to have! You continue to go, but each time the style is just not up to par with what *you* want and what you *know* she can probably do. She is just not seeing it as you do. I am willing to bet that you'd find yourself a new stylist without hesitation!

So why do we keep pouring energy (or money?) into possibility? You can see it, feel it, and know it all day long. But if your partner doesn't *also* see it or has a *different* vision, then you're falling in love with that temporary glimpse of potential you once saw that you wish to become a constant. After a while, the blame can't continue to be placed on your partner. He has shown you the present while you keep harping on the potential. Unfortunately, the only blame game that can be played is on yourself. If that person as he has been and how he is does not match up to your expectations, then let go with love.

One of the reasons people find themselves continuing to go back and answer the call of the past is due to chasing this potential. Maybe *this* time things can be as good as I want them to be. The cycle repeats and repeats because who's to say that the potential won't come to life the next time you go back? There is a lot of responsibility to bear in deciding to stop giving chances, because again, what if? Yes, relationships can be hard and fall off track. Growing pains are natural. But potential cannot be confused with growth because potential is stagnant, growth mobilizes. Partners can grow together, create visions together, and transform together. But they key is that it has to be done *together*. By waiting for the potential to materialize, we are actually holding ourselves back. A partnership is as strong as the weakest link. You want to reach new heights, but your partner is anchoring you down and preventing you from aligning your vision with your reality. I'll say this over and over again— if you can see it, you can have it! Meaning this partnership you desire is out there, you just aren't aligned to receive it due to remaining in the bubble of potential. Pop that bubble, sis!

Washington, D.C.

BOOMERANG OR IT DIDN'T HAPPEN

"Don't lose what is real, chasing only what appears to be."

Unknown

Over the last 10-15 years, dating norms have been totally restructured. Technological advances with texting and social media as the primary sources of communication have been the culprits in transforming dating and relationships. Before, people were not connected to each other 24/7. They had to utilize verbal communication and develop social skills through human interaction. Dating around was the norm! Nowadays, saying the word "dating" instead of "talking" when two people aren't in a committed relationship is basically the eighth deadly sin. We use the term "talking" to mean halfway commitment, and it's not uncommon for the talking stage to last indefinitely. Going on dates with multiple people makes it tricky when we're all in constant contact with one another not only via phone, but even on social media. It's common to make our moves known on social media, so the idea of ambiguity in the stages of getting to know people has gone out the window. On the flip side of that same coin, having multiple options at our fingertips readily available deters people from settling and committing to one person, and reinforces the forsaken gray area.

Digital connection has nearly wiped out the organic evolution of human and spiritual connection between people interested in one another. We get to know each other via digital means and wonder why actual human interaction can feel so foreign. We can see when someone is online, has read our message, or is even in the process of typing a message. We have endless options right from the comfort of our own personal devices. From behind a screen, we can fill emotional voids by engaging with an unlimited number of people, rarely connecting beneath the surface level. Our messages are overly thought-out, lacking the organic flow of conversation due to fear of judgment and protecting our image. This is modern dating in a nutshell.

They say this is the age of global connection. When it comes to the dating scene, are we actually connected? Or are we attached? How can we connect when we have this hyper-idealistic view of partnership that can be replaced at any moment when expectations fall short? We aren't connected to people. We're attached to their access to us. Connection is heart-centered and flows. It's authentic and unmasked. It's more of an energetic or spiritual spark. On the other hand, attachment has a more forceful tone, a tighter grasp. We're all aware that relationships have evolved over time from proximity based with the purpose of family building, to being more about love, loyalty, and romance. Relationships are no longer for practicality purposes. There is nothing intrinsically wrong with that, but having expectations for the perfect match in a partner paired with replacements so readily available makes for a giant mess. Why commit when something better may be out there? These are the unintended consequences technology has on interpersonal relationships.

Whether we like to admit it or not, it's rewired how humans interact and get to know one another. I wish I had a widespread solution to the digital barrier we have between us. On the micro level, we just have to be aware. Is the image we portray of ourselves on social media congruent with who we are in real life? Has conversing via text actually had an inverse effect on our communication skills? Are we afraid to be ourselves? Do we even know ourselves authentically? Ask the questions. Answer them honestly. We can't expect something to grow and flourish if the foundation hasn't even been laid. Technological advances have done wonders for us. But when our inner world has to be hidden behind a screen, we're sending a message that we are not comfortable with who we are; that we can't prosper without our digital shield of armor.

WORTH AND VALIDATION: DEFINED

"The real difficulty is to overcome how you think about yourself."

Maya Angelou

Self-worth is a concept presented to women from a young age all the way to adulthood. I always thought I had a decent understanding of this seemingly simple idea. *Yea, I don't hate myself so I have self-worth.* Wrong… Self-worth and self-love are so overused, yet so incredibly under-explored. The concepts are plagued with ambiguity, and only ever touch on the surface level. Self-worth is more than being comfortable with who you are. It's valuing yourself enough to demand proper treatment, avoid unhealthy circumstances, remain authentic, honor your inner being, and walk away from anything or anyone who threatens or undermines this value. Self-worth is learning to say yes to yourself, even if that means saying no to others. It's knowing and owning the dignity bestowed upon you simply from *being*.

While I never struggled with self-hate, I have learned that the alternative by default does not necessarily mean I had a strong sense of self-worth. When I was 17, I was in a relationship that ended up being a verbally and emotionally abusive situation. I treated him like gold. I treated him how I wanted to be treated, but I also treated him how *he* wanted to be treated. We fought horrendously. I never knew when the next explosion would occur. He would ignore me, accuse me of absurd things, and be downright mean. More times than not, I was an emotional wreck. After almost 3 years, I finally had enough and decided to let go, and let go for good. This was a pivotal moment on my reflection on self-worth. I stayed because I could not fathom how someone could treat someone so terribly when I was always so good to him.

It went back to how my normal was completely disrupted, and I didn't quite understand how to interpret it. I allowed his words and actions to affect me to the core. I knew I was not a bad person, but what I didn't know was that I was sabotaging my value by remaining in a situation where someone had the control to emotionally destroy me. I look back now with a few thoughts: *What was I thinking? Why did I ever allow someone to make me feel like that? I will never put up with anything remotely similar to that ever again.* The earth-shattering feelings that he would evoke from me then now seem so ridiculous to have ever even been entertained. But I was young. I was not used to dysfunctional relationships, yet dysfunctionality soon became my norm. I did not understand self-worth enough to know that I was not holding myself to my highest value. People who haven't been in a situation like that often cast judgment. I used to be one of them, until it happened to me. It's a slippery slope, and once you start down that hill it's extremely difficult to climb back up.

While I have never found myself in another relationship like that one, I did end up in a battle with self-worth years later with Damien. I have a strong sense of self. I know I treat people well. I know that my worth goes beyond physicality. I know I have a giving heart and an inquisitive mind. I know that I am a good person because I work at it every single day. So how did I manage to stomp all over my own self-worth? One answer: I was constantly trying to prove it. Damien saw it, but he didn't really appreciate it. It was as if I was constantly showing myself and doing things to illustrate how much I cared for him and how much I enjoyed treating him well. I was basically jumping in front of his face with a sign saying, "HELLO! DON'T YOU SEE?" It was exhausting. Draining and exhausting. He would tell me how other women he encountered lacked values and he was looking for someone with good values and self-respect. Again, hello, right here… So how was this a complete violation of self-worth? Because instead of moving away from him, I responded with a proof-driven approach. I wasn't being heard. I wasn't being seen. Naturally, I felt the need to show it more and more and more. Self-worth is acknowledging that inconsistency is consistency. It's knowing that if you aren't heard, nothing you do will make you be heard. A person who wants to see you, keep you, hear you, will do just that, without you having to over-exert yourself. I have developed two mantras to clearly explain how I failed to recognize my full value:

1. *What I would never do to someone else, I was doing to myself.*
2. *What I would never do to someone else, I was allowing to be done to me.*

Self-worth is acknowledging the patterns. If you've ever had pets or observed animals, you'll know exactly what I mean when I say they are creatures of habit. They live by routine. When anything, no matter how big or small, gets out of place or is out of the norm, they notice immediately. It's fascinating! They really can be great teachers. As humans, we definitely pick up on shifts in pattern. We know when someone's energy is off, or behavior is out of the ordinary. What we do with that information is where self-worth comes in. We often ignore the patterns or repaint the red flags. We sugar coat and attempt to rationalize our way out of what just *is*. It's not only keeping us in something we should feel validated in moving on from, but it's also belittling our own capacity to perceive the world around us. We can't control changes in patterns, but we can and must appropriately respond to them.

So, who defines it? Who defines our self-worth? We do. And since we define it, we are accountable for it. As living beings, we are born with dignity and shall always demand it. But we have to be careful not to confuse self-worth with self-entitlement. No one is without fault, and that's okay. I once wrote a heart-felt letter to my future self about not falling into a trap of maltreatment by others. I came upon the letter years later, and the last line has stuck with me since— "You are not perfect, but you are worthy."

    Self-worth cannot be void of self-awareness. If one does not have a constant awareness of his/her core values, humility, weaknesses, shortcomings, and personal growth, self-worth can easily become self-righteousness. The need for growth is not a sign of inadequacy. By neglecting to improve ourselves we shut the door on Universal blessings. We cannot demand from the Universe what we ourselves are not exhibiting. By this, I mean that if my motives and intentions are always selfish or impure, or if I am dishonest and hurtful towards others, I am not valuing that person and therefore, cannot expect my negativity to be valued. I will not receive what I want because I am not projecting what I want. We get what we put out. As simple as it sounds, it is a concept that we all need to frequently remind ourselves of.

Rome, Italy

FORGIVENESS

"Forgiveness is the fragrance that the violet sheds on the heel that has crushed it."

Mark Twain

Forgiveness is something that may never be sought, but must always be given. It's not an innovative concept. We have all heard the cliché saying: "forgiveness is about you! Not the other person!" And yes, it's cliché for a reason. But as always, if the idea of why and how the path of forgiveness is so critical is never explored in its depths, then its value becomes severely overlooked.

Forgiveness is a release of toxic weight— the feeling of pain that manifests as a solid block in the stomach and chest. Emotions have physical responses. It actually becomes unhealthy to harbor the aftermath of wrongdoings. I used to wait for an apology. Sometimes the apology came, and other times, it didn't. While an apology is a decent gesture, the apology itself does not always rid the harsh sentiments. Yes, apologizing is the right thing to do. Always. But the point is, someone asking for forgiveness does not automatically grant it. Forgiveness has to come from within. We ultimately choose to release or retain. By awaiting the apology, we place the power in the wrong hands. The one who hurt us *still* has control over our feelings and well-being.

  I had to forgive Damien on my own. At first, his apology was more of an "I'm sorry you found out this way, it didn't seem like a big deal at the time." I was obviously not comforted by that response, and after a week of internally sulking about it while I was in Greece, I decided I had to let it go when I got home. "Universe, as hard as this is, help me genuinely forgive him. I don't want to wish him ill will or have hard feelings, I just want to release this heaviness. I hope he has learned his lesson and reflects on his treatment towards others." As mentioned before, I begged the Universe for a sign. A sign that he had understood the depths of his choices. "I don't want him to ask for me back, I just want to know that he is aware and working on personal growth." The day did come. But the key here is that I forgave him *first*. I freed myself instead of waiting for him to be the liberator. Imagine if I had begged for the sincere apology and never received it. How long would that gut-wrenching feeling have lasted? And this is why the choice is ours. We have zero control over the actions of others. If we begin to live our lives contingent on the composure of the people who have hurt us, we forfeit our unique purpose and placement on this earth by being chained to the potential or lack of decency of others.

We physically, mentally, emotionally, and spiritually cannot move forward in our purpose while carrying such weight.

The topic of forgiveness in relationships is always a highly-debated one. And it is often surrounding the tumultuous issue of cheating or infidelity. There is no need to discuss the damage and destruction caused by cheating. The foundation of loyalty and trust totally crumbles. Although cheating is *always* wrong, there is *never* one driving force behind a person's choice to do so. What I mean is that there are the serial cheaters, the cheaters who seek what they are not receiving in their current relationship, the cheaters who had a one-time lapse of judgment, etc. Aside from the serial cheating, couples often struggle with what to do after the cheating comes to light. While some have a zero tolerance for it, others may try to understand the underlying cause and see if keeping the relationship alive after the remorse is a viable option.

I am not here to judge or give a blanket statement on what to do. But I will say this: consider your style of forgiveness. If you choose to forgive, you have to choose to not continue to hold the offense against the other person as ammo. You cannot bring it up when you're feeling insecure; you cannot put limits on your partner *because* of what happened. In choosing to forgive and rebuild, you're choosing to release. Will you bring this up or feel anxious every time your partner is out of your sight? Or are you confident in your forgiveness and rebuilding the trust? You have to really be honest with yourself. On the other hand, however, if you forgive but also know that you absolutely cannot trust again, then it is imperative that you remove yourself from this space. You are entitled to forgive, but not feel safe or comfortable in continuing to build in partnership with this person. And *that's* what absolutely has to be considered when trust and loyalty have been severed.

Forgiving others is necessary. We have to do it. But we also have to forgive ourselves. In my opinion, this is actually more difficult than forgiving someone else. Here, we first have to accept that we messed up. As grave or minor it may be, swallowing the acceptance pill is never easy. In our minds, we can alter or belittle the situation in order to cushion our conscience and our ego. But no. Rip the Band-Aid off with force and say it out loud: "I f*cked up." After we let that one out, it's time to apologize, and then it's time to exhale the cloud from within.

1. We can't go back in time.
2. We can remedy the situation with an apology, etc.
3. We can learn and grow by turning the lesson into a blessing

I have thought about times when I have hurt people and what I should have done differently. I also have to consider how I've let myself down and forgive me for harming me! Sometimes these thoughts can be haunting! The blessing in disguise is that these shortcomings have made me more aware. I learn from them, grow from them, and do my best not to repeat them. With pure intentions of despair for what I have done and a personal oath to let it build me instead of destroy me, I make the *choice* to forgive myself.

I have to share one of the most touching spiritual lessons on forgiveness and healing by the amazing spiritual teacher, Caroline Myss. Read her books and listen to her speak if you haven't already. She explains how the mind is not the tool for healing, but the soul is. To further make her point during a speaking event, she asked the audience to imagine someone who they have not been able to forgive. She urged them to really lean into that toxic feeling. Then, she told them to imagine that person coming up to them and saying something along the lines of, "Woah, bummer, I'm sorry. I never meant to hurt you, but hey can we just call it a day?" She confidently took a swing at it and presumed that no one actually felt any relief from that kind of apology, specifically referring to the part about not meaning to hurt the person.

In the next scenario, she has the audience imagine a different kind of approach from the person who hurt them. "… I need to tell you something. I consciously knew what I was doing. I sinned against you. I heard my conscience tell me not to do it and I didn't listen. I know my actions redirected the course of your life… And how much it hurt you did not stop me. This is not an apology. I am confessing my soul to you and am asking now for your forgiveness." Wow. When I heard that, chills went down my spine. She ended with saying *that's* how the sword gets taken out of the soul and heals.

This was such a pivotal moment in my awareness about healing. Forgiveness really is the vehicle to heal the deepest of cuts. Now, I know that very few people in this world would ever have the level of consciousness necessary to ask for forgiveness in this way. But something really profound happened when I fully participated in her visualization example. After imagining the soulful confession coming from the person who still had such a grip on my soul, I actually felt a wave of comfort come over me. Deep down we are not only hurt by that person's actions, but also by their choice in carrying out those actions. Her words cover those bases. I'm not sure if she intended for this example to be used as a technique in self-healing, but what a gift it has been. It really has the power to unleash the heart's glow, to sew the wound of the soul. Try it try it try it! You deserve to feel the warmth and glow of the light of the soul shine through you again.

Sicily, Italy

PROTECT YOUR ENERGY

"Do not let the behavior of others destroy your inner peace."

Dalai Lama

There is nothing more important for our emotional and spiritual well-being than protecting our energy. Energy is magnetic. It is a force. Energy transfers constantly, and without caution, the wrong energy can pierce through us like a roaring storm— knocking all parts of us down in its path. Friends, coworkers, or even family members can threaten our energetic flow. Know your triggers and set boundaries. It's okay to cancel plans when you feel your energy has been overworked. It's okay to avoid certain people whose presence drains you or gives you anxiety. It's okay to say "no" when too much is being asked of you. Anything or anyone that puts you out of alignment is a hazard to your energy. Energy is frequency; it's vibration. Toxic energy disrupts this flow. Your vibration lowers, in turn, causing your mood and emotional state to dwindle as well.

Protecting your energy is protecting your sanity, your spirit, your peace. Cleansing your space is crucial. Physical, mental, and spiritual health are dependent on shielding yourself from any and all unnecessary threats to your energy. Sometimes, though, toxicity creeps in. It comes in many different forms. And sometimes, it can take time to really identify the harmful effects of having such toxicity up close and personal. Toxicity doesn't discriminate against any type of interpersonal relationship we have. It's easy to target the energy vampires, the hard part is putting up the shield.

I'll start with the toxic family members. These can be quite difficult to navigate because it's kind of hard to just not be that person's daughter/brother/cousin anymore. For some people, minimal to no contact works with the family dynamic. For others, maybe not so much. For those who have to see or spend time with the dreaded family member (s)— boundaries. Boundaries absolutely have to be set. Maybe it's a situation where being around your parents drains your energy because of bickering, an unhealthy environment, or outright disrespect. It's okay to draw the line *even* when it's a parent. Maybe you need to set a clear and non-negotiable boundary of one call a week, or one visit a month. Whatever works best for you and your newly committed self in energy protection mode. With family comes the feeling of obligation. For children, there is less autonomy in boundaries and keeping distance. But as a full-grown adult… well-being comes first. No one is obligated to bear toxic weight because of relation— blood or not.

I had a friend whose mere presence sent my energy into turmoil. She was superficially pleasant, but under the surface was a deeply troubled individual. She lied all the time. She would talk terribly about everyone behind their backs, and then make plans to hang out with them soon after. She would lash out at completely inappropriate times, and her fake and inauthentic character made me quiver. Even a text message from her would have me feeling uneasy. It wore me down enough and I had to take control of my peace. To be honest, "toxic friendship" was a concept I never really understood in the past. Why would you be friends with an energy-sucking vampire? Typically, it doesn't start out as bad. But over time, the ugliness slowly peaks through. By that point, you feel too invested. Or you have too many mutual friends. Or at times it's fun to be around this person, and other times the thought of being stuck in a shark tank seems more tolerable.

Healthy friends and friendships don't drain you, repeatedly do you wrong, or have you questioning their morals. The best thing to do— cut ties. The hardest thing to do— cut ties. You don't want to have the "break-up" talk with your friend because you're not dating. So, what is there to do? The truth is, if someone is a threat to your well-being, makes you feel worse more than they make you feel good, or causes anxious feelings to arise, then distance, space, and boundaries have to be established. It doesn't need to be a loud production or announcement; we are all entitled to moving in silence. You don't owe an explanation when it comes to honoring your gut instinct and protecting your peace. It may be awkward at times. But awkward is good. Awkward will keep that person at a distance as most humans try to avoid awkward situations. Stand firm in the awkwardness until the final cut has been made. Once it's done, don't fall into the trap of starting a smearing campaign. Maybe this friend was only toxic to you, but their energy works with other people. Or maybe other people haven't had the chance to see this person's raw and true self yet. Rest assured that the truth always and forever reveals itself. Just stay in your lane and keep it moving.

And now for one of the worst forms of toxicity—toxic relationships. The added romantic and emotional elements create a perfect storm for remaining in these situations for far too long. Toxic relationships are incredibly complicated because no two situations are ever the same. For some, it begins rocky. For others, there is a gradual move from seemingly healthy to ugly and dysfunctional. I will say with a good amount of confidence, though, that the red flags that are ignored early on are almost always a foreshadowing of what is to come. *When people show you who they are, believe them!* We have a tendency to excuse the little things, and by the time the big things enter the scene, we are far too emotionally invested to make the rational decision to leave.

Toxicity manifests in a variety of ways: your partner dimming your shine, you questioning your worth, questioning trust or loyalty, gaslighting, physical abuse, verbal and emotional abuse, silent treatments, irrational accusations, frequent and excessive fighting, deceit, and many more tactics involved in tumultuous relationships. However, sometimes just having a feeling that something isn't right is a sign that the relationship is not authentic. Just make sure you aren't projecting past traumas or having anxious thoughts to create the "off" feeling. Trust the vibes you get. If it doesn't feel right, it's because it's not right. Sometimes our bodies alert us to toxic energy, and that feeling is actually a way of the body rejecting this person's energy. Listen to your intuition! But, of course, the rocket science part is not identifying the toxicity, it's *getting away from it*. Here's the thing, it doesn't get better. There may be moments of hope, but that's just it— they are moments. Healthy, thriving relationships are built on consistency. There is a solid foundation and when problems inevitably occur, the structure is not in danger of collapsing. Toxic relationships, on the other hand, are barely held together without excessive force. If something is not flowing, it is not for you. Accept the harm for what it is. Painting a pretty picture of the situation does nothing but buy some time. Turn to a support system. It will be a painful decision, but pain is not synonymous with wrong. Remove yourself and don't look back. Let the hurt flow through you. It's normal to feel hurt after a breakup! Know that your worth has been severely undervalued and now is the time to re-establish your standards. Staying in something that the depths of your core know is not right blocks you from the blessings that the Universe has in store for you. Learn from it. Grow from it. Protect your peace physically, mentally, and emotionally. And trust that by protecting your worth and your energy, you'll eventually attract a partnership that matches your frequency, not stifles and depletes it.

By protecting your energy, you're protecting your peace. Some of us are incredibly sensitive to energy and can be drained very quickly. There have been countless days where toxic energy has infiltrated my system, causing a plummeting effect to my vibration. One of the most crucial things to do is to physically remove yourself from the space. But how do we shield ourselves from the non-physical interactions that come catapulting towards us? When people say or do certain things that really just jeopardize our peace. By this, I mean when we are not physically in the room with an energy sucker, but this person is still in our zone of contact. These days, energy can 100% be transmitted through a text message or even *the lack* of a text message, for example. I used to absorb it all— feeling totally enraged or hurt. One day while dealing with an episode of negative energy absorption, I decided that I needed to move differently. I wanted to have the power over my own energy. I have no control over what people do or don't do. I only have control of what I allow into my zone. And so, one day, the answer to protecting my energy dawned on me.

    You know those trendy fabrics that repel any absorption or stain? The commercials will show someone pouring red wine on a white table cloth, and there is absolutely no permeation. Fascinating. I had this vision of a plastic, umbrella-like shield around me that would inhibit any toxic or unwanted energy from disturbing my peace. I first tried it when that old friend still had such a grip on my energy cords. I took a breath and envisioned the shield. Her negativity was just plastered to the outside and slid down like a melting ice cream on a scorching summer day.

I became the observer, not the absorber. I slept like a baby that night. I felt so grounded, protected, and empowered. Let me tell you that envisioning this bubble has been life-changing! Trust me, writing it and saying it aloud made me question my sanity, BUT it has been the most freeing method of protection, and the least exhausting! It really only requires a vision in the mind. It can be done anywhere, at any time, and I highly recommend giving it a try. Or at least exploring your own way to enter protection mode because this sh*t works! And it's totally necessary.

Shielding is not meant to substitute healthy boundary setting. The reality is that without complete isolation or reclusiveness, surrounding energy has the potential to disrupt our own, and we need to have the tools in place to protect ourselves. Energy is not only transmitted through personal interactions. It's transmitted through nuanced means of communication, social media, and verbal conversations. It is even transmitted through silence. Unfortunately, we can't physically remove ourselves from all of these things. The energy bubble allows us to keep our energy pure, and more importantly, to know that the power in protecting our sacred energy lies within.

THE SUN, THE MOON, AND THE TRUTH

"The number one principle that rules my life is intention. Thought by thought, choice by choice, we are cocreating our lives based on the energy of our intention."

Oprah

The power of the Universe is something that can't be denied. Energy circulates as a magnetic force. Our energy flows into the Universe, and it would be foolish to underestimate the implications of not only our energy, but surrounding energy as well. It is through this energy that the truth manifests. We can use words and actions to hide these truths, but the intentions are organically transmitted through our energy. Processing such energy is an evolutionary skill we possess as humans.

How often does one's intention not appropriately align with words and actions? I can think of my own shortcomings. When we do a good deed, is it being done out of the goodness of our heart, or for recognition and the notion of "getting something in return?" Our energy communicates the true intention behind all we do, say, and believe. We have to keep our intentions pure, void of any negative ulterior motives. It reverts back to this inner truth that we have a duty to live by. We've all been around that person who gives us a compliment that somehow doesn't give us that warm and fuzzy feeling. It's most likely because the intention behind the comment wasn't genuine and we were able to pick up on it. Words matter, but so does the intention behind those words.

Intentions can absolutely get misinterpreted. We can do things purely from our hearts and still be met with backlash or criticism. This is because people can only meet us and perceive us as deeply as they've met themselves. Consider a time when something was bothering you and your intention was to bring the issue to light in order to resolve it. That may fall on someone else's ears as an attack, or as intentionally being negative to start conflict. Maybe their emotional and communication skills are on a different level than yours, and they can't fathom how uncomfortable conversations can be healthy and constructive. Still, intentions should be set honestly and wisely.

It's also possible that our intentions are pure, and we actually do end up hurting someone. In this case, we don't get to dictate or police that person's feelings. Just because we did not intend to hurt someone, or don't agree that what was done was hurtful, having pure intentions does not grant the permission to invalidate someone else's perspective of reality.

    We have to be masters of intention. We have to keep intention at the forefront of all we do, think, and say. It is the navigator of the reality we are creating for ourselves. It would be silly to believe we can deceive the Universe. The truth is carried in intention, not necessarily in action. We also have to trust ourselves and our abilities to interpret the energy behind intention without sugar coating or making negative assumptions. That's a hefty burden to face. We just have to get it right. Listening to that energy is a skill we have in our tool box of life, and we can't let it get rusty.

    The hardest part is applying that skill objectively, even when we are in situations that we desperately do not want to be bad for us. We've all done it— talked ourselves out of the flight response. But guess what? The Universe is relentless. We can ignore the gut feeling to the point where our own energy has been depleted, our spirit dimmed, and our rationality continuing to suppress our innate ability. That is until the Universe slams the truth in our face, making it impossible for us to try to wiggle ourselves out of the inevitable. Without intention, action would essentially be meaningless, free floating. Intention steers us to and through our reality. We have to listen as best we can when the Universe speaks to us via intention, and we absolutely have to be calculated and genuine in projecting our own intention. Energy doesn't lie, and eventually, only 3 things come out: the sun, the moon, and the truth.

New York, New York

DESTINATION HAPPINESS

"Happiness is a state of mind, not a set of circumstances."

Richard Carlson

Destination happiness is dangerous. Circumstantial happiness is equally as dangerous. Yet, I have unknowingly been doing this my whole life. "Life sucks right now, but once X happens it'll be fine." Wrong. Destination happiness is when your happiness is based on outside or future events or people. So, why is this so bad? Well, any time our happiness is based on "other" or "outside" circumstances, we are setting ourselves up for imminent failure. I have done this so much that I basically have had to recondition myself to drop this dead-end mentality. This is what my destination and circumstantial happiness has looked like:

"If I get into that college, everything will be perfect!"

"If I can land this dream job, everything else that sucks

right now will suck less."

"Once I pay off this credit card, I'll be golden!"

"If he could just communicate with me better, I'd feel so much more assured."

"Once I figure out exactly what path in life I want to take, my happiness will be achieved and no one will be able to ruin it."

The danger! What happens when I don't get into that school? When that dream job actually isn't all that dreamy? When communication improves one day, and drops off again the next? Happiness has to be a mindset and it's not easy. I don't mean that once you discover that happiness is a choice that absolutely nothing can shake you up. No, we are human and have emotions. However, the difference is that without a solid foundation of a content mindset, you will find yourself in a constant battle of temporary happiness followed by inevitable disappointment. You have to be content with your life when you're broke, hurt, and have no clear direction. Read: *I have to be content with my life when I'm broke, hurt, and have no clear direction.* The dream house could burn down. The love of your life could leave you. You could be let go from your job. And if happiness is tightly attached to any of these circumstances outside of your control, you automatically set yourself up for failure. Happiness does not have to look like smiles and laughter; it looks like a steady and serene calmness, where positivity always wins. I don't mean positivity in the sense that you will always get what you want, but rather it is knowing that what does happen is always for the highest good. Ultimately, happiness is a choice. We are so used to attributing happiness to materials, achievements, or people, that we fail to realize how much control we actually have. We have to exercise the ability to *choose* a healthy mindset daily, especially in the wake of adversity or disappointment. It takes practice. As always, the first step is awareness. Be aware of the power of the mind, then make it a point to choose your own happiness— whatever that may look like.

I have let *myself* down countless times with having the conventional standard of happiness-achievement idea. It came to a point where I realized that even when I got the job I wanted, took a dream vacation, or met a great guy, I still found myself sunken in a hole of unhappiness when any of these situations did not hold up to my ideal version of them. Even when I had these things and another aspect of life became crappy, the "happy" was gone. I had to make a change. I made myself aware of this damaging habit. Any time I tell myself, "I'll be so happy if..." I know that I have to stop and reflect. I need to be content now— without my desired destination, with the possibility of my desired circumstance never arriving.

Do you catch yourself doing this? The answer is most likely yes. And that's okay! Don't panic; you're not doomed. Now you might be more aware of how you have done this or continue to do this, and we should never underestimate the beauty and power in awareness. Like most other personal development nuggets, the most difficult part is always accepting that our own lifelong ways of thinking have been essentially keeping us caged or in some sort of high to low cycle. "Unconditioning" what we know feels like an insult to our whole life! That's why embarking on these spiritual or self-growth journeys *sound* like some fairytale adventure, but *feel* as if each new revelation is a wave knocking you down with another one coming before you can get up! We've all been *that* person at the beach, being tossed around the shore, hair in face, bathing suit floating 10 feet away… so you know exactly what I mean. Disrespectful if you ask me. But it usually makes you a better swimmer and you have a story to share for a lifetime. Win-win!

Destination happiness also teaches us to be happy now, in the present moment. I suppose the word "happy" makes people weary. It's not humanly possible to be happy and giddy every second of every day. As I said before, happiness is whatever *you* make it. It's simply being content right now, and optimistically hopeful for the future. Being content in the moment could look like enjoying your morning tea or coffee. Savor those moments. There will always be a million things that have to be done, or attended to, or fixed. The happier you are now, the more clarity you have to face those "things" later on. Are you more productive in panic, high stress, and irritability mode? Or are you more productive when you're grounded and calm? Rocket science, I know.

One of the biggest obstacles for people is holding themselves accountable when it comes to relationships. We absolutely cannot share ourselves or make our happiness dependent on anyone else until we are fully and unwaveringly happy with ourselves and our circumstances. Without having that inner stability first, it would be a form of self-sabotage to wait and have happiness depend on anyone else. It makes me cringe when people say "you complete me" when referring to their significant other. I don't mean this in a judgmental way, but it actually concerns me. It exudes this incredibly unhealthy idea that fulfillment comes only when paired with someone in a romantic relationship. It's desperate and forceful, not magnetic and loving. If things go badly, are you no longer complete or whole? No. We were born whole. A healthy, thriving relationship is not when two halves make a whole, but rather when two equal *whole* parts form a union of badassery. Where it is a partnership in power, and not a partnership in dependency.

On a train somewhere, Italy

ROMA ROMANTICIZED

"Finding your true self is kinda like looking for sunglasses that have been on top of your head the whole time."

Suzanne Heyn

Roma, Roma, Roma.. Rome happened after about a year and a half in the making. The idea shot to my mind after the life-changing trip to Sicily I took in the summer of 2016. My spirit was lit up. My soul wanted it. The plan was that I would move to Rome temporarily to teach English. I always wanted to teach, and was in love with Italy, so it was almost a no brainer. However, fear and skepticism were not far behind. I could envision myself there. But then all of the *hows* crept in. How will I afford this? How can I do this alone? How will I be able to find a place to live? How will I get around? Being a few months out of college, I was still living at home, and once the discouragement from my parents entered the scene, my shaky desire vanished into thin air.

A year passed and I was dangerously unhappy with

my job. I was in a 9-5 setting that was stifling and toxic. The environment was not for me. It shattered my childhood view of growing up and aspiring for the 9-5 office job. My "normal" was completely disrupted. I hated every second of it. It was around the time that I was hardcore struggling with Damien, and on top of that, I dreaded getting up every morning to go to work. I would tear up on my way to the office and often times even while sitting at my desk. It sucked my energy dry. I needed a change. And I needed it fast. If you have ever felt invalidated because of a feeling in your soul that your workplace or current occupation is a source of unhappiness, let me tell you that you are completely entitled to this feeling. Work is necessary, but suffering is not. Get out!

After returning from Greece, it was go time. My spirit was being renewed, and so was life as I knew it. My friend and I decided that we belonged in Europe. We took online courses around our full-time jobs to become certified English teachers. And we set the plan in motion to move to Florence, Italy. This time, I still had my doubts, but I also had this unwavering desire to get the f*ck out. We would leave January 2nd. *New year, new me heyy*. I say this with the utmost conviction when I tell people that had I not had the opportunity to quit my job and move, I would have ended up institutionalized. I was absolutely not okay. I was damaged— mentally and spiritually. I hated what I was doing. I felt so unfulfilled and unaligned. I was in the process of rebuilding emotionally. The environment had to change.

Shortly before we booked our trip, we were strongly advised to change our destination to Rome instead of Florence due to job opportunities. This was sort of the first taste of going with the flow and trusting the process. The day came. We set out with our one-way ticket to Rome. I had such high hopes! I had this ultra-romanticized view of how my experience would be. Here it is: After finding a job and a place to live, I would be settled down and whole again. I would be on this journey of finding myself. I would sit in quaint little coffee shops in the heart of Rome writing my book, meeting inspiring people, and having enlightening conversations. It was a full-on soul-searching escapade. My travels would be exhilarating. After 6 months, I would come home a totally new woman. Unstoppable. Let's get it, self!

But here is how it actually went. I share with you a Facebook post I wrote giving everyone an update of our first two weeks abroad.

Hello friends and family. Kelly and I have officially survived our first 2 weeks abroad. The blog will follow, but here is a recap of our time so far.

If it isn't already apparent, moving to another country comes with countless unforeseen obstacles. It began for us in the airport. We eagerly walked up to start the check-in process, only to discover that half of our bags were double the weight limit. So, in front of an audience (the 50+ people standing in line) we were forced to open all bags and reorganize our items... a major shout out to our families for jumping into crisis mode with us.

Our flight was great. We arrived in Istanbul for a quick layover and were seated at our gate awaiting departure. During boarding time, we did not see anyone else sitting near us. We quickly discovered that our gate had been changed last minute... to the complete opposite end of the airport. We were unfortunately "those people"... SPRINTING through the airport with backpacks and luggage. We made it, though! Another obstacle overcome...

Once we arrived in Rome, we took a deep breath of fresh air. WE MADE IT!!!! On our way to our Airbnb, we were so thrilled to be able to relax. The cab driver had a friend in the passenger seat, which we found to be odd, but we just wanted to get settled. During the drive, the driver abruptly pulls the shuttle over on the side of the highway near another vehicle. Kelly and the other young female passenger began to panic and scream, asking him what he was doing. In true European fashion, he was only dropping his friend off with this other vehicle (while on the job), but Kelly was convinced we were in a real life Taken situation.

To add fuel to the fire, we nearly called a cab to take us back to the airport to go home once we saw where we would be staying. Picture this... we arrive at the location to meet our Airbnb host to get the keys. The area was more horrifying than can be explained, and we begged the cab driver not to leave us. He left anyways. Our host and his friends carried our luggage across the street to the apartment. One minor detail left out of the reviews section was that in this one-bedroom abode, the host lives there as well during the stay, and sleeps on a cot in the living room. To add some spice to this experience, he informed us his lady of the night would be joining him that night. We called our best friend in tears. We stayed up until 6am searching for another place to stay, and as soon as the sun came up, we dragged all 400 pounds of luggage down 4 flights of stairs out onto the street to trek to our new place. Finally, after 3 Ubers canceling on us, a kind man on the sidewalk, observing our distress, gave us the number to call a cab. We laugh uncontrollably now, but at the time, the tears were flowing. We ghosted our host.

    Our new place was great. The food in the area has been amazing. It is quite possible that we drink more wine and espresso than water... and we may or may not make a daily trip to the bakery for cookies... We were so fortunate to start our jobs less than a week of being here. So now all that was left was to figure out the transportation system. While neither of us use this method of transportation at home, here we are in a foreign country attempting to make our way through a brand-new city. So naturally, the first bus use turned into an hour and 45-minute commute, instead of the breezy 15 minutes it should have been. This may have also happened the first time using the train...You gotta learn the hard way! Keep in mind that neither of us have data plans and are left to our own devices to navigate through this wonderful city.

Another thing they don't tell ya is how tricky these Italian doors are to unlock... This led us to be locked out of our apartment for 30 minutes before we contacted the landlord begging for help. He sent someone over, but unfortunately for this kind man, the key magically worked seconds before his arrival.

As much as we have struggled, I am so happy to be here. We work with the Ministry of Defense teaching English to high ranking Naval officers. Each individual has a different language proficiency level, and we are tasked with creating lessons specific to their needs. For the more advanced students, I get to teach English through the use of articles and reports on international and political topics. Anyone who knows me knows that this could not be a more perfect set up....

We still aren't completely settled, but we have come a long way from crying in a room together, contemplating returning home. We can't wait to be able to start traveling. More updates will follow.

Needless to say, adjusting to life in Rome was not at all the romantic view I had previously envisioned. The rest of the trip was uncannily similar to those first two weeks. Anything that *could* go wrong, *would* go wrong. Including, but not limited to: multiple Airbnb escapes, contracts on housing falling through, finding a scorpion in my room, being temporarily stuck in Morocco with no information on how we would be getting back to Rome, and having to scale a fence and run through a swamp in order to make my train on time. Don't get me wrong, we had some incredible experiences. We were traveling through Europe for goodness sake! But the constant (and I mean constant) bout of bad luck was exhausting, discouraging, and often left me bawling uncontrollably. It was so bad, that one morning our contract on an apartment fell through and we had two hours to find another place to stay before literally being put out on the street. But in the end, everything that had gone so horribly wrong, *always* ended up becoming so beautifully right. This proved itself so many times, that after a while, I stopped panicking in the face of adversity. I just *knew* that something better was to come. If there was one thing about Rome that changed me to the core, it was this. Honestly, now whenever shit hits the fan, after the initial freak out, I sit back so grounded and so convicted in knowing that the Universe has my back. So, thank you, Rome, for constantly having me on the brink of losing my own sanity.

The theme for my own spiritual growth has centered on intuition, and actually *listening* to it. I bet you're wondering if we ended up being put out on the street or not after a lease agreement falling through the morning of move-in day. So here it is: no, but almost. After extending our stay at the temporary Airbnb twice, we really had to crack down and find a permanent apartment. We had two days to do this. Two days! Desperation was kicking in. We no longer had the luxury of being "choosy." We somehow managed to set up an appointment to see an apartment in a fairly good location. We walked in, and immediately everything inside of me was telling me to run. There were 6 people with 1 bathroom. The apartment was falling apart. And we would have to share a room. The landlord also wanted a crazy amount of money upfront in cash as a security deposit. If there ever was a time for logic to overshadow intuition, it was now. We had no place to go. Logic was screaming in our faces: ARE YOU REALLY ABOUT TO TURN DOWN A PLACE TO LIVE IN A FOREIGN CITY? AND SLEEP WHERE? ON THE STREET WITH ALL 18 PIECES OF LUGGAGE YOU HAVE? WOW SO SNOBBY OF YOU, HONESTLY.

My mind was telling me to just shove this intuitive response under the rug. We left to go withdraw money. Neither one of us wanted to say what we felt. But by the grace of all that is good, we looked at each other and just said, "No. We can't." And we didn't. We decided to put up the blinders and go sit in a bar with Wi-Fi to continue the search. When I tell you that listening to your intuition is for your own good, believe it! As we sat there, we connected with another expat looking for roommates who just happened to find an apartment with 3 bedrooms and 3 bathrooms. Near a metro. Incredibly affordable rent. No room sharing?? No hostel like living conditions?? The Universe was directing us there the whole time. But imagine if had we let logic and desperation trump that gut feeling. We would have blocked our own blessings.

Of course, we can't go back in time or know the other side of "what if," but how many times have you done something your whole body was rejecting because there was no logical reason to deny it? Or out of fear of looking stupid for following a feeling rather than a tangible, logical map? Here is your validation to trust that feeling with your life. You don't need to be able to explain it or put it into words. You don't need to verify it or prove it to anyone else. And you most definitely don't need to surrender to your own battle between mind and intuition. It's the retroactive mind versus the proactive intuition paradigm. Your mind will only tell you what it already has been exposed to; intuition will guide you to what has yet to be seen.

I went to Rome to find myself. To escape my lifeless way of living back at home. Through the darkness of every crushing obstacle, through the exhaustion of constantly being on the move with work and travel, through accepting that my romanticized fairytale was not my reality, something amazing happened. I realized what the rest of my life would not look like. It wouldn't look like working tirelessly for other people, and it wouldn't look like making decisions based off of fear. After this experience, there is *nothing* I can't do. I didn't find myself. I *aligned* myself. I discovered my inner purpose buried under years of conditioning from conventional societal ways. I realized that life is not at all about finding who you are, it's about discovering who you were always meant to be. "Finding" actually means aligning and discovering. And then creating your way. Too often we have this idea that we need to search far and wide, ahem like moving to Rome, to find ourselves. But all along, we already have everything wired within us. It's when we're out of alignment that we feel "lost" and the desire to "find" enters our brain space.

Rome was yet another prime example of "destination happiness." And as you can see, it failed in the sense that it did not match up to my fantasy. Moving to escape problems, or thinking that a new place will all of a sudden be the cure to closing open wounds, are really good ways to experience the exact opposite. It's imperative to be happy *before* changing scenery. I don't mean happy as in you're living a perfect life with everything you've ever desired, but being content with the now. Remember, happiness is a mindset. It's not a place. It's not a person. It's not a job. It's perfectly acceptable to feel connected to a place and envision your life in that place to be further aligned with your purpose, but it's totally fruitless to be miserable in your current space and holding out for or romanticizing the next. Take your happiness with you and enhance it; don't chase it once you arrive.

Washington, D.C.

THE ART OF NOT REACTING

"La verità è come un leone. Non avrai bisogno di difenderla. Lasciala libera. Si difenderà da sola."

Sant'Agostino

Silence is power. It's often louder than words, and exerts less energy. Win-win if you ask me. Silence was never a strength of mine, though. As a child, my most repeated behavioral offense was back-talking. I couldn't just shut the hell up! I had to get my point across. It carried with me. I have no problem speaking my mind, or telling someone off when they've done wrong. It's not always a bad thing. Our voice is a tool; being heard is necessary. We often use our voice for those who don't have one. But sometimes, we need to zip it.

It is an art. We need to be silent when expending our energy will be ineffective in the end, when someone has done us wrong beyond repair, when someone is invalidating our thoughts and feelings, and when we have already said what needed to be said. You know when you get SO angry and all you want to do is create a novel or verbally ream the person out about how they're wrong and you're right and how and why can't they understand this?? Yea, perfect time to hit 'em with that silence. Not everything needs a reaction. Being selective is paramount in energy protection. Silence often conveys what words cannot. With silence also comes a removal. You can't not react to someone being shitty over and over again, but remain in the same space. No! Silence is sort of the last straw. No reaction is a loud reaction. Reacting with the pent-up rage, harboring the anger, expressing the anger to the equivalent of a brick wall, leaves you where? Even more angry than when it began! Certain people and situations do not deserve the energy or time required in combatting their perceived reality.

The art of not reacting takes a front seat on the journey and path to a spiritual awakening. The whole point of an awakening is to soar through this new realm of consciousness. But the thing is, not everyone can come along for the ride with you. It's a shift in life where discovering oneness with the Universe, or Source, is a riveting experience, but is not experienced by all. Relationships and friendships that were superficial, or merely tolerated, have no room in this brand-new arena of growth and awakening. Quality over quantity proves itself here. It is not at all that you are now almighty and above certain people, it is just that you are now in a totally different *lane*. With this movement comes a lot of confusion and negativity from those who feel this drift. They do not have the same awareness, and will remain in their comfort zone. They will also talk mad shit about you. Here is where the silence comes in.

One of the most difficult things to process during this transformation was knowing and feeling the spewed negativity from the ones who I veered away from. I did not miss them; I worried about my reputation. I knew they would try to tarnish my character with lies and hate. It made me want to make sure that the people in their circle knew I was not some evil self-righteous person now. This was my ego coming through. The ego can appear in a very logical manner, but one thing the ego cannot do is operate from below the surface; the soul can. I also remembered intention. And how truth is *always* revealed. You have to operate in love, with pure intentions of elevating yourself and not elevating your ego. In silence, there is serenity. I don't have to protect my image because the Universe does it for me. Anything done with love, receives only love. Anything done with deceit, receives just that. Truth has an all-encompassing power. It circulates with force, trampling over the fake and ugly energy with ease.

So, please, sit back in silence. Know that the Universe is forever in your favor. Pure spirits and energy will be drawn to you. Simply wish the ones left behind well, and keep it moving. And *never* halt your journey out of fear that someone else's lower, toxic frequency has any type of chance against your loving, sky-rocketing vibration. That's like stopping at McDonald's when you're on the way to Ruth's Chris; quick and easy, but then you feel shitty after.

Washington, D.C.

LET THE GOOD THINGS END

"Suffering is trying to rise before the fall.

Pain is necessary, suffering is a choice."

Pema Chodron

Living abroad didn't always have me stranded somewhere, or crying in a bathroom. Some really, really great things happened, too. At the end of the Roman adventure, the friends I was with and I decided to spend the last month we had abroad in two of the greatest places on earth— Sicily and Crete. We started in Sicily. I remember the moment I spotted him. It was almost like a movie— I look over and see a sculpted bronze god relaxing alone on the beach. He had just gone for a dip in the water and came out literally glowing. As the day went on, he moved closer to where we were sitting. Our two other friends joined us, and before we knew it, the four of us and a group of his friends were all playing beach volleyball.

I'm about to bring you on a real-life Kostas and Lena *Sisterhood of the Traveling Pants* experience. One night, Alex and his friends made plans to take us out. Before we went out, I sort of didn't want to go. To be honest, I had a feeling that something in the romance department was on the horizon and I wasn't sure I wanted to see how it would play out. I vividly remember being in the hotel room after getting ready and saying to the Universe, "I trust your plan." We all went to dinner and had a great time. After, the kind gentlemen took us to a bar in another city. It was time for some cocktails and dancing. I was having a fabulous time! As the night played out, somehow Alex and I locked in on the dancefloor and the rest was history. Universe, ya did it again! Without any force on my part, he made his way to me.

We all spent the remainder of the trip rolling deep as a crew. Alex was such a kind soul, so thoughtful, and so generous. To my surprise, there was more to him than just his incredibly good-looking appearance! Us girls left a few days later for Greece, but being on a high of spontaneity, my friend and I decided that after our time in Greece, we would return back to Sicily for a short time before having to go home to the U.S..

I really noticed how special he was while I was in Greece. His communication was flawless. For me, communication has been such a divider in the past and this was truly as if the Universe was finally placing what I had been seeking in my lap. The best part was that he did it without me having to ask for it. I was so excited to see him again before having to return home. That time with him showed me even more what a special person he was. How did I get so lucky? I *never* get this lucky. We both had experiences in the past that shaped us into how we treat others, and knew exactly how we wanted to be treated. We balanced each other and created a sense of security.

I came home for a month to resettle and await the arrival of my niece. I had plans to return to Sicily at the end of the summer because I knew some family and friends were going, and now, there was even more of an incentive. So, during that month that I was home, we both knew I would be back in five weeks. At one point, the rationalist in me said, "Look, I know we are far apart, but if your feelings happen to change, please just have the decency to be honest with me." In a nutshell, he explained that he was very interested, but obviously, after my next long trip, we would have to evaluate the situation in order to see if there would be a future between us. He also was concerned that he would be working more during the time I would be there and wouldn't be able to give as much of his time to me as he did previously. Of course, I understood completely. We might as well see where this goes because we could both feel the connection between us. If all went well, this could be *really* good.

The second-best moment of the summer (the first being the arrival of my niece, of course) that I had been waiting for had finally come— time to return to the motherland. We didn't see each other every day. This time around was much more relaxed and low-key. After a few times of seeing him though, I could tell something was off. I felt a certain distance even while in the same room as him. It was nothing he did, but the energy could be felt. I knew he was exhausted from working every day and what not, so I *decided* to attribute it to that. Towards the end of the trip, I had reached the point of being ready to talk about the inevitable. We sat down at a coffee shop and I said, "So what happens when I return home?" "I don't know. I've been pulling back because I knew this time would come and it would be easier to part if I had refrained a little." *Ah-ha, I was right!* I told him that I noticed his cooler demeanor, and what he said next sort of rocked me a little bit. "Distance for me is not an option. I care about you, but I don't know what the future is between us and I don't imagine it to blossom after you return home. If I happen to meet a girl in the future that I am interested in then I will go forward with it." *Cue the hard gulp to hold back the tears.*

"Oh. Ok. Understood." We continued our conversation because me being me, I need to know the rules here. Do we continue to talk when I go home? Do we say goodbye on the final day and leave it at that? It was all unknown. What we wanted couldn't happen at that moment. For me, meeting someone overseas was no strange concept. My mother and my aunts all met their husbands while vacationing in Sicily. I've seen it firsthand. Again, it was my normal. We were both struggling. The next day he called me. I could hear in his voice how defeated he was. He said that he knew he liked me, but had not realized *how much* he liked me until that point. We decided to see how our fate would play out. The time to say goodbye came through like a hurricane. I bawled. I also bawled in line at the airport to check in, on the airplane, at every layover, and when I finally made it home. Meeting someone you really, really like who lives over 4,000 miles away is so fun, people!

    A little over a week of being home, I once again had to address his sudden energy shift. He said that he didn't know how to carry himself. He missed me, but we both knew the reality. I then asked him about coming to visit. He said that he was unsure if it was something he could do. I prompted more and told him to remove the idea of if he *could* and tell me if he *wanted* to. "As much as I want to, I can't. Your feelings are stronger than mine and if I came there, they would become even stronger and after I would feel bad. I have no idea what my future looks like." HOLD UP. I don't know what measurement was used to calculate this, but that was my time to go into protection mode. "If you think my feelings are stronger, then we shouldn't continue to talk." He wanted to keep in contact, and see what would happen. I was reluctant, but I gave it a shot. About a week later, there was yet another shift. It was again more of a feeling that came over me more so than anything he did. One night, I found myself in my room with tears streaming down my face. Something wasn't right. It brought me back to the days with Damien, where I was consumed with this head-to-toe feeling. I vowed to never ignore that feeling again, even if I had no concrete answer. I'm a strong believer that we are faced with the same hardship until we get it right— until the lesson is learned. This was my round two with having that unshakeable feeling. And also, this proved to be another affirmation on how energy transfer has no boundaries (we were literally in different time zones on different continents). This time, I needed to rely on myself without layering it with questions. I wanted to honor and trust my inner guidance. Even if I wanted to be wrong, the knowing was far too strong.

The next day, as I sat in a coffee shop after work waiting to meet with a friend, I told myself I had to address it. Part of the feeling I had was that someone else was involved. I did not want to come off as accusatory, but I told him that we couldn't continue to talk because the reality was that we were really only talking until or while he met other girls. "I have to tell you something, too," he said. Aw, hell. Why does it always have to be me prompting the truth to come out? And so, he began to say that a few days prior a girl he met previously had contacted him and he could potentially be interested. This time, we really had to cut ties. We were both hurt, but it had to be done.

Here are the golden nuggets of this experience. Something seemingly good had to come to a close because of outside circumstances. And that's okay. But the true gem lies in listening to my gut. As hurtful as it is to know that someone you really feel a connection with could be interested in someone else is as enjoyable as being stomped on by an elephant. However, there was an ounce of me that was sparking with joy. I listened. I took it in to my own hands. I protected myself through honoring my inner wisdom. I was even more certain of how much of a treasure intuition is. The physical response I felt could not be ignored. In the past I have ignored it with rationalization, with thinking of alternatives.

And so, the next step was grief. Raw, unmasked grief. There is no right way to grieve, but there are plenty of wrong ways. Pain happens, but suffering happens when we try to skip the pain, rush the pain, rationalize the pain, mask the pain, suppress the pain, or try to avoid the pain. I allowed the hurt to flow freely through me, to take its course. Pain can sometimes be interpreted as, "This is wrong. I have to fix this." We go into crisis aversion mode. Like addicts who go through withdrawal, emotional pain is very similar. We feel that we absolutely need another fix. The good news is that in cases of lost love, we actually don't *need* another round in order for the symptoms to subside! In the past, I would mask hurt by going out, or thinking about the next guy who could come along, or even telling myself it was his loss and he'd miss me. I acknowledged that I wanted him, but I also knew that what is meant for me won't pass me. There is a greater purpose behind unfortunate experiences. Days prior to having things come to a full stop with Alex, I kept seeing posts online about the importance of letting go. I mean, multiple times a day! One stood out: "Give people time. Give people space. Don't beg anyone to stay. Let them roam. What's meant for you will always be yours." I saw the signs. I treat these as the way the Universe offers guidance. If you are open to the signs, they are always there.

I have to leave you with one last thing. Never give false hope. But it is equally as important to never accept false hope. In the following days, Alex would message me saying he was upset and that I was on his mind. He also repeated that he didn't know what the future held for him, and that maybe one day we will be if it's destined. Pause. No. I have done this. I cringe thinking about it. I have said it partially meaning it, but mostly trying to ease the other person's emotions. Now, I can't speak for his motives. But I can say that I had to nip that future talk *real* fast. While I had no resentment or ill will towards him at all and I wasn't holding on to a thread of hope to see what the future held, the reality is that it is a dangerous trap to fall into. Yes, maybe one day paths do reconnect. But in the present moment, no one knows when or if that is in the cards. I feel as if he meant well, and I do have respect for him because of how honest he had been, but I knew it was necessary to put up the barriers against the false hope.

We have to thank the Universe for these experiences. Sometimes the good ones let us go, and vice versa! Not all endings have to be hate-filled and hostile. We should be able to honor the divergent paths, while still having an appreciation for the pleasant experience. Let the emotions flow through you, and then remember with the utmost conviction that what is for you will be drawn to you. We eventually learn to celebrate these stepping stones because honestly, the best is yet to come.

FROM REJECTION TO REDIRECTION

"Rejection is an opportunity for your selection."

Bernard Branson

Rejection is ugly, y'all. We hate it so much, that we sometimes avoid putting ourselves in situations out of fear of rejection. I'm talking about rejection in all forms— from being dumped, to being fired, or even being told "no" when asking for a favor. Personally, rejection was incredibly uncomfortable. It elicits feelings of inferiority, of not being good enough, or of not being cared about. Hold onto your seat before you read this next sentence: now, I LOVE rejection!

Rejection is arguably one of the most amazing gifts the Universe can hurl at us. Here's why: rejection removes us from situations not meant for us, *and* the decision is made by something or someone else, so we don't have to endure the dreaded inner battle of deciding for ourselves. Magic. I know what you're thinking. "Well, crazy lady, what about when I get rejected from people or places that I actually enjoy and find to be good for me?" Oh, silly one, you may *think* that, but the Universe has greater plans..

When the universe blindsides and sucker punches you, you can either lay in your bed sobbing for an indefinite amount of time, or you can do that for five days and then redirect that energy into something meaningful and purposeful. That is what I have learned and love to do—redirect the turmoil to growth and comfort through mind expansion and expression. It sounds loaded, I know.

Anyone who has gone through the heartbreak rejection, already knows. It sucks. It's unimaginable. It can't be right. But it happened. We can't change it, and chances are we shouldn't change it even if we could. And let's be clear, I didn't have my heart broken and then that day decide it would be a good idea to put into practice this notion of "redirecting energy." No. I sobbed for days. Even weeks after I would have a meltdown. It's our natural emotional response, and if we didn't feel that way after being heartbroken then we'd all be sociopaths or something along those lines. As horrendous as it is, it comes with the territory of being emotional beings.

So how do we redirect this energy when all we want to do is crawl in a hole and disappear? Unfortunately, we don't all have the luxury of being Taylor Swift and make millions from our heartbreaks. But we can enrich our lives in different ways. What is your passion? What brings you pure joy? What changes have you been wanting to make?

When the Universe Speaks

They say that after a heart shattering break up, many people make drastic changes in their personal lives. But what exactly causes this transformative response?

When I lived in Rome, I'd often be so caught up in the day to day chaos that I'd forget to just step back and soak it all in. I was living in a city that was once the greatest empire in the world. The mastery and genius put into designing and constructing Rome and the Roman Empire continues to leave historians in awe. As enchanting as Rome is, it can be equally as tantrum-inducing and frustrating. One of the most nonsensical aspects of the city was the transportation system. There were only two major metro lines at the time to manage the hustle and bustle of millions of locals *and* tourists. It honestly baffled me how such a tourist trap could have such poor transportation. And then I learned a thing or two. There had been various construction projects to add new lines, but the projects would be stopped in their tracks (pun fully intended) a majority of the time. This was because that whenever the digging commenced, historical artifacts would be discovered underground. Once that happened, all digging had to stop and archaeologists had to be called in. This unearthing process revealed historical gems, the essence of ancient Rome, that had been buried under layers and layers of modernization.

After getting through my dramatic episodes of throwing a fit about the transportation situation, I began to understand the parallels of Rome's unearthing to my own— to the unearthing process people go through in the face of adversity. Life, as we know it, is susceptible to disruption at any moment. In a flash, our walls of normalcy and comfort can come crumbling down. It applies to any situation that bears a storm, whether it be heartbreak, job loss, losing a loved one, or any other traumatic experience. When we get so unbearably shattered, the shell cracks open. Our inner pieces get revealed in the most raw, pure form. During the process, layers of conditioning start to peel back, or unveil. We slowly begin to access the depths of the soul. The parts of ourselves that have been buried have made way to the surface, no longer cloaked in all *other* truths we have piled on along the way. It is in this moment that we should look to grasp the beauty in adversity.

    The seeds are ready to be watered and nurtured. We can take this experience and turn it into blooming season, or we can try to sew it back up. Our lives have been molded and programmed since day one, so peeling back the layers is no quick task. But allowing the unearthing process to be the catalyst for radical shifts in mind, body, and spirit connects us deeper with ourselves by giving us the wholly uncovered view of who we are at the core. It is by divine structuring that after becoming so tragically unearthed, we can utilize that time to become so beautifully rediscovered. In the midst of dealing with the emotional responses that are inevitably paired with soul crushing situations, the unearthing brilliantly sparks a push in us. A push to make those radical changes away from the societal conditioning stacked upon us. Unearthing redirects us to our divine purpose, or purposes. We feel the importance of disconnecting from that which does not genuinely honor our inner being. Connecting with the innocence and pureness of the soul puts us in that "feel good" state, or flow state. It's vulnerable, yet freeing. It's how we start living on purpose. One of the greatest revelations in all healing journeys has been to get to the next phase of empowerment. It is empowering to fully know the strength of the mind, body, and spirit when the unthinkable happens. Recognizing unearthing as a stepping stone to being so deeply in tune with yourself is exactly how we take the reins of power and begin to operate from our own truths; it's how we empower ourselves to face any future setbacks with grace. We unlock authenticity and throw the key away. Unlike the Roman excavation, there is no need to call in outside reinforcements. Be your own archaeologist and asses your own significance and value upon discovering the magical treasures awaiting to shine through you. *That* is the key to living our absolute best life.

After Chris, the redirection manifested in reading inspirational books I never would have previously read, pursuing a career change, committing heavily to fitness goals, *and* writing this book. After Alex, the redirection took form in creating my very own business and vowing to work for myself in the future. It was magical; creativity flowed through me abundantly. I had a clear vision of the life I wanted, and now knew how to make it happen. These events were crucial in pushing me towards aligning with my inner purpose. I don't find any of this to be coincidental.

Whether we acknowledge it or not, the universe has it all lined up. Remember, I thought both of these guys were good for me. But sometimes the Universe knows that we're selling ourselves short and it takes a crumbling experience to push us toward where we are meant to be. Without the breakups, I most likely would have not only been complacent with the day-to-day, but I also would not have had the spark to put my fullest potential into action.

While I was in Rome, I had to start thinking about employment opportunities for when I returned home. I was so unbelievably fortunate to be hired by a company in Washington D.C. to teach online while I was still away. When I returned, they asked me to take on a few different teaching tasks for in-person classes. I was so grateful, that I almost felt unworthy. I absolutely loved my job. And after basically depleting my savings abroad, it was beyond necessary for me to be working. After a few weeks, I realized that another teacher and I were placed in competition for a full-time position; something that was never told to me upon starting. The other teacher caught on too, and so began his road to sabotage. He would constantly approach me and say things like, "You should really teach abroad again." "How come you're not teaching abroad?" "Are you teaching anywhere else currently?" I would even hear him telling his students that he was better than the other teachers. He was in my boss's office daily, a** kissing away. I spotted his conniving motivations immediately and began to distance myself from him and the company. Being near him was becoming unhealthy.

Competition in the workplace has never appealed to me; and that is one of the biggest flaws that the professional world forces upon employees. I knew that with my retreat and the fact that he had more teaching experience, they would eventually choose him, and they did. I won't lie, at first, I was angry that they didn't see how ingenuine this person was. My ego was bruised, but my spirit was relieved. I surprisingly had a sense of calmness come over me. The Universe had my back. I loved this job. But it was no longer my why, or my passion. It was a temporary means to an end. Remember, energy transfers. My heart and soul were somewhere else, and so the decision to fully shift my focus to where it belonged was made for me. It comes to show that even when we resist the inevitable, we eventually get put in a position to take the leap out of the comfort zone or to keep pouring energy into the wrong things and wondering why we feel so unfulfilled. I had been putting off my personal work and book writing because of the job. While they still offered me online and private courses to teach, my hours were cut. The Universe knew that if I continued putting all of my time and energy into teaching, that I would fall very behind on fulfilling my true purpose— creating my online business, writing my book, and traveling often. Losing a job would normally send me into a rage or psychotic break; but this was different. I already had this appreciation for rejection, but one of the ultimate tests in trusting rejection is when it comes to your financial well-being.

 Rejection serves as the catapult we need to be

steered in the right direction. It's the propeller we need when we fall out of alignment. I love to think of the bow and arrow analogy. We first have to be pulled back in order to be launched great lengths. All that happens to us is only to serve us. We can't fight it, though. We end up blocking our own blessings when we fight against the current. Let it go, and let it flow. The art of the let go is life-changing. When someone or something walks out, let it. Don't chase it. Don't stifle it. Simply wish it well. I can promise you that if it leaves you, it is not meant for you. Once it's gone, keep it in the past. We have a tendency to bring our past to the present by reliving the dreaded experiences in our mind. The thoughts alone fire off the same neurons that were released at the time of the incident. We have to stop physically and chemically knocking ourselves back.

One of the main reasons we get so hung up and bent out of shape after some sort of hurt is because of our egoic response. Deep down we know that if something is not working in our favor or the other person's favor, then it makes sense that it should cease to move forward. The emotional investment totally sucker-punches our ego. Often times we can look back and be spiritually aware of why something turned out the way it did, but in the *moment* we feel as if we've undergone some form of attack. "He left me." "They fired me." "My friends betrayed me." These are all universal protections, yet we feel so hurt because of the emotional attachment; our ego feels less than. We have to recognize that the ego is the sole driver of emotional turmoil after rejection or loss. It is a chaining mechanism rather than an aid to staying the ever-flowing course of the spirit. Allow spirit to be the guide because I promise you that surrendering to the waves of life opens portals. I emphasize the concept of "allowing" because being open to receive after rejection is critical. If you stay so completely focused on the past and what is now gone, you totally miss the road signs to get you to your next destination. After rejection, practice the following:

1. *Accept it*
2. *Embrace it*
3. *Open yourself*
4. *Receive*

You will be so glad you did!

Washington, D.C.

POWER HOUR

"And, when you want something, all the universe conspires in helping you to achieve it."

Paul Coelho, The Alchemist

You probably get the sense that I'm on team "You Create Your Own Reality." We are taught to believe that our reality is dependent on our environment or outside circumstances. It makes total sense— we are reactive beings. Or so I thought. I used to absolutely loathe the "change your mind, change your life" crowd. What does that even mean?? Well let me tell you exactly what it means.

Maybe you have heard the saying, "what you focus on grows." Or that your thoughts become your reality. It all comes back to *drum roll please* energy. Energy is frequency. The vibrational frequency begins with our thoughts. When we think happy thoughts, we emit high vibrational energy. Adversely, when we're in a low mood, we emit low vibrational frequencies. As energy is a magnetic force, the energy of the Universe meets us at these frequencies. The Universe is an energy field. Yes, of course the Universe is always and forever working in our favor, but only when we *let it*. For example, Sour Sally has been single for a few years. She believes that all men are liars and cheaters, and does not understand why she can't find a wholesome dude. Whenever she goes out, she takes this "men are trash" energy with her. She also brings it with her on her dating apps, on the metro, and out shopping on the weekends. So, what kind of men are making their way towards Sour Sally? You bet ya, the crappy ones or none at all. Her negative, low expectation vibration is being matched!

What if she, instead, acknowledges that she has come across some of the less desirable men out there in the past, but has this knowing and this trust that good men do exist. That her wants, also want her. That the man she is manifesting, is also manifesting her. She creates the condition to put herself in a space to see and receive wholesome partnerships. Don't believe me? How many times have you spilled your coffee all over your work clothes on your way to the office, screamed and cursed what a terrible day will ensue, and then that terrible day actually *does* follow? If you can't quite get to the point of thinking of yourself as this mystical being capable of creating reality, then just understand the basics. Energy is magnetic. Low frequencies attract low experiences, and high frequencies attract desirable experiences. It comes to down to perception. Perception is a major factor in understanding the thoughts to reality paradigm. Low, pessimistic frequencies force a shift in perception. Sour Sally with her "woe is me" attitude perceives the world in a negative light. We really only attract and perceive as much or as little as we allow ourselves to. Negative attitudes cause our scope to narrow in on everything that is wrong around us instead of everything that flows so abundantly. By contrast, with pure energy operating from the heart space, we allow ourselves to see the beauty of the world in everyday life. When our thoughts radiate with optimism and trust that the Universe is a source of ever-flowing wisdom, then we begin to perceive an abundant reality. Positive thinking is not at all living in a fantasy world, but rather it's trusting that whatever does happen is only to serve our highest good.

You may be wondering how does one even begin to raise their vibration and create, or manifest, the life they have only dreamed about. It starts with a morning ritual. How you spend your first waking moments, or the "power hour" as I like to call it, map out the rest of the day. This is where the intersectionality of gratitude and manifestation comes into play.

I can, of course, share what has worked for me, but the idea is to tailor a routine that fits *you*. However you decide to implement your routine, I highly recommend incorporating the following:

1. Meditation
2. Journaling

3. Personal Development

I won't dive deep into the nitty gritty of meditation because so many others do it way better than me. But meditation is life-changing. It's restorative— down to the cellular level. It's rejuvenating. And no, it does not have to entail sitting silently with your legs in a pretzel position with zero thoughts going through your mind. It's refilling the fuel tank because who can constantly run effectively on E? Meditation is the art of allowing Universal messages flow *to* you. Being at ease and mindful in the present moment is the optimal state to be in to receive clarity. Our focus during the day to day life always has to be on the task at hand, or the next step. Giving yourself the time and space to step back takes you away from the encapsulated stress zone, and into the broader arena of abundance. If your life is the on-stage performance, meditation is the backstage break; you're away from the fast-moving environment and restoring your energy. Retreating allows for a broader view to release stress, ask for guidance, and receive answers. Our best insights don't come to us when we're in go mode in the midst of all the noise.

When I first started dabbling in meditation practices, I had no idea what the hell I was doing. When I finally began to incorporate it consistently, my life drastically changed. My stress level decreased immensely, my sleep improved, productivity became more streamlined, and the clarity I had been seeking effortlessly began to flow to me.

I have fallen in love with the twice daily Ziva meditation

that incorporates mindfulness, meditation, and manifestation created by the wonderful Emily Fletcher. Her book *Stress Less, Accomplish More* is a must read! The goal when turning to any wellness and self-help book (this one included) is to add tools to your tool box, but also to fully understand and feel confident in trusting that you know what is best for you. You are your greatest resource! Find a meditation that works for you and your lifestyle before automatically dismissing the idea. You'll then wonder how the hell you ever made it this far without a daily meditation practice.

Journaling is unfortunately often misunderstood, especially for non-writers. Most people hear "journal" and think you have to write a "dear diary" prompt or fantasize your dream life. While it certainly can be that, I totally understand that not everyone takes the creative juices to paper. I came across a more practical approach to journaling that makes it less fantasy-esque and more relatable for people of all writing backgrounds. First, begin with any fears, uncertainties, or stressor s that are on your mind. *What has been weighing you down?* The physical transfer of what's weighing on you to the paper actually does alleviate some of the pressure. When we keep things bottled in our brains and hearts, we get cloudy, ready to explode at any moment. Transferring the stressors on paper creates space in our minds to think clearly, relieve some anxiety, and best-case scenario, seeing it on paper may reveal that the worries actually aren't *that* bad on their own without being paired with layers and layers of overthinking.

Secondly, gratitude. There is always something to be grateful for. It can be something major, or something as minor as a comforting, soft blanket. The best way to feel full is by appreciating all that you do have, instead of focusing on what you don't have. Additionally, gratitude extends to the things and experiences that haven't yet materialized. When you're grateful for what you don't yet have, you begin to start vibrating at a frequency of abundance— allowing you to invite these desires rather than being in resistance mode because they haven't yet arrived. Your energy frequency will match the frequency of the exact thing that you are manifesting! Before I launched my business, I had to energetically operate as if I was *already* a business owner with a clientele. By writing things down such as, "I am grateful for my clients. I am grateful for creating my own financial freedom," I started to bring those future desires into the present. I was becoming a magnet for my wants. It's powerful stuff! The essence of expressing gratitude is that it brings you to the present moment *and* raises your vibration. If how you start the day sets the tone for the rest of the day, then what better practice to kick off with than gratitude?

And lastly, goal setting. Your big long-term goals should be written and organized somewhere else. Here, it's more efficient to have the mini daily or weekly goals that build up to the big ones. Writing the major goals each morning can be daunting because focusing only on the end result leaves no room for appreciating and creating the little steps along the way. The goal for each day should be to get yourself into that flow state. You know when you just feel good for no obvious reason? When life is just enjoyable and bright? This is when it's easiest to go after all of the other goals we have for ourselves; when self-doubt has been drowned out by our soulful joy. Establishing a solid, "me time" morning routine is one way to get ourselves in this state of bliss for the day. The daily goals can be practical ones as long as each goal is getting you one step closer to leading the fulfilling life you deserve. Maybe it's a goal to finally get to the grocery store, or maybe it's a goal to start editing the resume for job applications you've been putting off. Whatever it is, get it out of your head and on that paper! Finally, get excited about these goals. These are your uniquely crafted puzzle pieces to living your best life. It shouldn't be an eye-roll to-do list. Remember, outside inspiration and motivation is definitely a booster. But the best and most profound inspiration can come right from the source— *you.*

Personal development is the golden ticket to self-growth and mind expansion. Taking a few minutes to read, listen to a podcast, or watch a motivational video is one of the best ways to immerse yourself into the topics that speak to your soul. It can be validating, encouraging, inspiring, and an opportunity to grow within that space. Check in with yourself. How's the mental? How's the body feeling? What do you have coming up? What areas could use an added dose of magic? This is *personal* development— not for school, or work, or projects. Often times when we introduce ourselves or engage in small talk, the most common question is, "so what do you do?" Sure, that's important. But then we get caught up in our identity being attached to what we do or even what we don't do. Personal development is a way to tap into your inner being. To begin to identify yourself from within, rather than from the external factors. Ask yourself, "who am I?" If you're speechless, don't get scared. Get pumped! Now you get to go on a deep diving exploration of who you are, why you are, and what keeps that authentic you sparked and full.

I began the chapter explaining that a solid morning routine is a critical step on the way to manifesting the life of your dreams. Manifestation is seeing and feeling your way into your future self, so I've boiled the manifestation process down to three steps. I like things in 3s, have you noticed?

Step 1: The Vision The vision is that "thing" in your mind that you want but feels so distant and abstract. Well, anything you see you can create. Get very, very clear on this vision. Take notes on it— be as detailed as possible. Holding it in mental view is powerful on its own, but creating a vision board that you can physically see daily is next level. The key is to keep this vision front and center! If it's hanging out in the back of your mind leisurely, it sends a message to the Universe that it's not really that important to you. Edit your vision and vision board as needed. Do not be afraid to think big! Nothing is too grand to bring to life, so take it to the lengths and depths of your heart's desire. In this stage, most people psyche themselves out because they fear being judged or ridiculed by other people for taking their desires seriously without assigning a "reality check" to them. Ignore it. It's your vision, not theirs. They can't see it. People cast judgment on things outside the realm of their consciousness. Keep in mind that judgments only have value if you assign them one.

Step 2: Belief You must believe it exists *and* believe it's already yours. We can all daydream about beachside living on an island in Greece. But do we all believe that it's actually possible? We should, but social programming kicks in and reminds us to stay within bounds. Your vision has to be so picture-perfect clear that you actually feel yourself in that space. You have to begin to carry yourself in the *as if;* as if you already have it. As if your vision board is your reality. As if you are experiencing these desires in the present moment. Feeling your way into it is major. But of course, it has to be paired with action! You may not know exactly how everything will fall into place, and that's perfect because the how part is not your job. Your job is to lean holistically into it— mind, body, spirit— and ask yourself what can be done in the present moment to get you one step closer to transforming the vision to reality. Each step, no matter how minor or significant, is equally as powerful in terms of inching you closer to blooming season. Use present tense affirmations, act on it tenaciously, and breathe in the energy of creation and adventure. You've got this. I promise.

Step 3: Evolution Let it evolve. I think this is where it gets tricky. Having the vision and belief kickstarts the process. But we have to understand that the mind is actually limited in scope. We base our desires and perceptions based off of things we know to be true and exist. The Universe is limitless, infinite. What often happens when the vision begins to change direction is that we get discouraged and perceive it as failure. In reality, it's just the vision evolving to serve our highest good. A couple of mistakes can be made in this process. One is that we become so laser focused on our version of what the desire looks like that we fail in being receptive to superior Universal guidance. It's like zooming in on a tree and blocking out the branches from our viewpoint— branches of opportunity and abundance. Another thing we do is suffocate the vision to death. We hold it so tightly in our grips that we do not allow any room at all for it to flourish and grow. Think of it as trying to plant a bouquet of roses in a Tupperware container. It physically cannot happen! The key to the evolution of manifestations is to surrender. Surrender to the infinite wisdom of the Universe. Surrendering is not at all an apathetic cop out, but rather a sacred trust and acceptance that the Universe gifts us with our soul path, and not necessarily the path of the somewhat egoic and limited mind. Getting redirected or rerouted is by no means failure. Sometimes while driving we come up on the dreaded "detour" warning. We can either surrender and trust the detour in getting where we need to go. Or we can ignore it by keeping on the preplanned route only to be up against a dangerous and difficult flooded area; or worse, turn around and go back home. Let me just say that when we fully allow ourselves to surrender, the reality tends to unfold in a manner way better and beyond what we could have ever even imagined.

Manifestation allows us to fully absorb the idea of being a creator rather than a planner. Creators have vision, but the manner in which the vision comes to life evolves organically with artistic flow. On the other hand, planning requires a step-by-step guide to achieving completion. How does evolution and surrender fit into a plan? It really doesn't because not sticking to *the* plan signifies that we messed up, we did something wrong. An artist at a canvas doesn't "plan" her piece, she creates it and lets it develop along the way. Just as we don't say that God "planned" the world in seven days, rather he created it. Manifestation is truly a beautiful process. But again, only if we allow it to be. The challenges and difficulties that come up are not nearly as daunting as the blocks we put upon ourselves. I found that in building my own business, the hardest part really had nothing to do with lack of business knowledge or the financial aspect of starting a business. It was the self-doubt, the limiting beliefs, and the fear. I mean, it was absolutely crippling and something I was not prepared for. I was anticipating all the difficulties with marketing, tax logistics, clientele, but none of that even compared to the subconscious creeping in to bring me back down to "reality." I had to dig deep and recognize this as negative self-talk stemming from a sort of cognitive dissonance. If we're not careful, the subconscious mind can deceive us and keep us small. The *conscious* mind, however, uplifts us to be more in tune with the grandeur of the Universe. Nip the negativity. Work through it even when you feel completely inadequate. Set the thoughts aside and invite the *feeling* of the achieved desire to steer you. If you don't, no one else will because this is *your* vision, and yours alone. You cannot rely on external validation; you might even need to expect the exact opposite. Unwaveringly be your own biggest supporter, co-conspire with the Universe in creating the life of your dreams, and watch how the powers of transformation were rooted within. Let them sprout!

THE MAGIC IS IN THE PRESENT

"You're doing amazing, sweetie"

Kris Jenner

If you're reading this, you've probably dabbled in spirituality and enlightenment to a certain degree. The saying, "the path to enlightenment is by being in the present moment" may not be new for you. One of the greatest joys I've had on my own journey is taking these "woo woo" sayings and illustrating how simple, yet profound they are in application. In the present moment, there really is no other state to be in than that of pure bliss. It's void of what happened prior, and what's set to happen next; of what was or what will be. We're not anchored to past worries and we're not being yanked to future scares. In the present, we just *are*. There is no greater moment of connectedness with oneself than in the present moment. In this moment, I am writing this paragraph. I am not bogged down with regret about all the time I wasted instead of being productive earlier, and my thoughts are not anxiously bouncing around about the heavy weight to-do list awaiting me. Is it normal to hold on to the past and anticipate the future? Well, of course. But typically, we're really only focusing on the negatives of each time frame. While the things we have to do next are not harmful on their own, stressing about them robs us of absorbing the beauty of right now. When is the last time you *just* drove? Or *just* took a shower? Without replaying that awful thing that happened yesterday, or the constant forward thinking of what's next? Focusing on the next is not productivity. If the present moment is freedom, then the relentless backtracking or anticipating is imprisonment.

I have always been a Nervous Nelly. The anxiety of always having something to do left me actually doing nothing as I trapped myself in the overwhelm. I had to really integrate the whole one step at a time thing. Before I went to Rome, the thoughts about what would have to be done once arriving kept me up at night sweating in fear. I remember one time snapping at myself and telling myself to just shut up already. Being concerned about which phone plan I would have to get once I arrived was serving me zero purpose as I was tossing around in my bed while still in *America*. In the right now, we can't pile on the looming credit card bill coming due. There is just nothing that can be done right now to stop that bill from being due. And guess what else, the bill just *is*. No, I am not condoning poor financial management habits, but how can one strategize with clarity if we're consumed with what's pending? Another prime example is a new mom I met who felt like she had no idea what to do with this tiny human. I gently nudged her to the right now. I told her how 10 minutes ago I had seen her feeding the baby, and in that moment, she was doing a pretty stellar job. I also brought her attention to her snuggled up, sweet baby sleeping in the carrier. "Right now, your baby is warm and resting. Sleep and warmth are essential for babies, so right now you *do* know what to do, and you're doing amazing." Does that eliminate new mom anxieties? Again, no. But coming into the present reinforces the *I am* and *I can* narrative that an overwhelmed mom so desperately needs as she's learning the ropes.

Our world is constantly on the move. Onto the next task, the next degree, the next promotion, and the list goes on. We no longer live according to our basic necessities. However, life is only ever in the now. We neglect and deprive ourselves of that experience when we constantly jump and skip mentally to things that have not even met us in the physical realm. We owe it to ourselves to just *be*. To be more present and to live more. Part of prioritizing the present is allowing ourselves to have moments of boundlessness. Where we do what we want for leisure, or fun, or we do nothing at all without any shame or regret attached to it. Burn out is real. Constant mental or physical movement is draining and throws everything way out of alignment. The power of the present lies in the fact that the past and future simply do not exist *right now*. Bask in the moment, powerfully restore in the present. Take a look around and simply celebrate all that *is*.

WHAT FEEDS YOU?

"The soul is covered by a thousand veils."

Hazrat Inayat Khan

What lights you up? What causes you to have that feeling of walking on clouds, fully content, without a worry or weight on you? I always thought that only the profound, spiritual gurus in the world had a "purpose." That purpose somehow was only valid for those who had the ability to make real widespread change in the world. If someone asked me what my purpose was, I would just give some generic response. I didn't understand it. It seemed abstract, and only meant for those who had global influence and exposure. "Yea, ok, there's no way every single person has a so-called purpose. We can't all be the Dalai Lama." Boy, was I smacked up against the brick wall between superficiality and awareness. Until that wall came crumbling down piece by piece on this path of spiritual awakening.

I guess that's where I should start. Spirituality. I

always thought that spirituality and organized religion were one in the same. But then how is it that people from all walks of life have gone through an awakening of sorts, down the paths of their own spiritual journeys? From different cultures, regions, religions, and so on. And that's when it dawned on me. Spirit is energy. It is connectedness. Spirit is the Universal force that binds us all together as one operating system. Some say Universe, some say God. It is only when we tap into this spirit that the gap in connectedness decreases. I like to think of it in terms of an enclosed circle. In the center of this circle is a beam of light, or the point of connection. The rest of the circle is comprised of us earthly beings floating around. When we gravitate towards the beam, we feel most in tune and aligned in purpose. We are achieving fulfillment.

Purpose is when we align as closely to this spiritual center as possible. When our being is flowing towards the center of connectedness, and not pulling away in resistance. That feeling of being on a high is the feeling we get only when we are nearing this center. And so, the saying, "everyone has a purpose" is not cliché, or reserved for the master teachers of the world at all. So how do we get this "feeling?" That feeling comes over us when an image or thought of what we feel drawn to comes to mind. Better yet, when we're actually doing these things as an extension of who we are. The thing that brings about pure happiness. Some people are drawn to writing, some are drawn to treating illnesses, and some are drawn to images of themselves on the red carpet. It's usually that seemingly distant dream that brings so much joy, but so little confidence or understanding of how to *get there.*

When we're born, we are wired uniquely with physical and non-physical traits. At birth, we already have innate seeds of purpose waiting to be discovered and watered. Purpose blossoms when we pair nurturing the seeds with removing blockages in order meet the conditions necessary to bloom. Purpose is that thing we have always been drawn to, or felt a connection with. Often times, even as children, people are drawn to their purpose. Of course, it manifests according to age and ability. I do not have the statistics, but I am confident enough to say that most people are born and die without ever tapping into this realm of fulfillment. We are conditioned to follow the status-quo. Straying away from the norm of success achievement will leave us homeless and hungry. Or so they say. We are taught early on that purpose is secondary to survival. Purpose is a hobby and has no place in the constructed pathway to success. You have a passion for art? Paint on the weekends! You love animals? Volunteer at an animal shelter once a month. If everyone lived their purpose, how would systems be maintained? How can we take a risk in living out our purpose when student loan debt is mounting over our heads? Modern society does not cultivate an environment rich in self-purpose. It simply does not allow for it. But who says we are chained to that design? The ones who break free and start living on purpose are the ones who ultimately reach the highest fulfillment.

I struggled with this. I was always drawn to connecting with and helping people. As a child, I wanted to be a teacher. Like every 7-year-old, right? As I got older, family and friends in my circle of influence filled my head with this idea of financial stability. I was discouraged from teaching, and pushed to aim for that ever-so-promising government job. I studied Criminology and Global Terrorism in college. I held various internships that I hoped would ultimately land me in a government agency. I even interviewed at a national security agency. Something hit me, though, and I actually didn't want to be one-dimensional and work for the government for 40 years. I, instead, took a job in the private sector after graduating. All through school and at that job, I was always drawn to leading study groups and offering to train or help new employees. I didn't want to be at my desk, I wanted to be at someone else's, showing them the tricks I learned along the way.

And then I actually *got to be* a teacher! One of the greatest jobs I've ever had. I loved teaching the material, but what I loved more was the meaningful conversations between the students and me. I knew I had always had this burning desire to educate and open minds. Society told me that to educate means to educate in an academic setting. What I discovered on my own though, was that my desire is actually to coach people. Coach people through the process of healing, or the process of aligning with their unique purposes. Life coaching is not an elective in high school, or a major in college. How would I have known how to properly align myself with work I am passionate about if I was never really exposed to it in the years of being molded for the "real world?" From a young age, I knew *what* I was drawn to, I just didn't exactly know *how* that would manifest in terms of service and success. It got to a point where I could not ignore this inner pull towards empowering people through healing and working for myself. I would bet my last penny on this— if you can imagine it, you can create it. The Universe is limitless.

I have noticed that people get really uneasy when talking about purpose. They feel that if they really don't know what their purpose is, then their life is void of meaning. It can be discouraging. Purpose doesn't always have to be one thing, though. It can be a way of life or expending your energy across multiple passions. Purpose also doesn't have to align with a source of income. I personally find the ability to have soul purpose and success coexist as one of the most soulful gifts we can tap into. But I also know that not everyone has that holistic approach. If you enjoy your job and view it as a means to be able to fulfill your purpose outside of work, then great. The point is to not feel entrapped in the concept of "more work, less play"— where working overshadows and stands in the way to the path of the beam. I realized how my own sense of purpose unfolded in many layers. I was first drawn to teaching, which led to my interest in training. Through teaching, I was more drawn to the human interaction as opposed to actually teaching content. It eventually clicked that coaching is very much a form of teaching. For the first time, I knew what it meant to align, and not grind. There's a reason I was chosen to be in charge of the "Advice" column in the middle school newspaper!

I urge you to dig deep. Or maybe not so deep at all. Maybe you know exactly what you are drawn to. If you are unsure, I want you to answer this question honestly: If money didn't exist, what would you be doing every day? That burning passion you have; the image of yourself in an ideal world— *that's* your purpose. The two greatest inhibitors of fulfilling a dream are fear and money. Let me just say, fear is not a stop sign and there is an unlimited abundance of money on this planet. Fear was my absolute biggest inhibitor— fear of the unknown, failure, and inadequacy. When I really considered why I was so fearful to gravitate towards the beam, I realized it was because it meant taking a leap out of my comfort zone. How can transformation and change flourish in an enclosed area? Fear is the bridge between our comfort zone and growth. So, in short, if you're afraid, you're teetering towards transcendence.

One of the greatest lessons about fear that seeped into my heart was from a restaurant owner who is the epitome of living on purpose. The restaurant was featured in a news segment for allowing the homeless to eat for free. I had a chance to speak to the owner, and his open arms extend even beyond the homeless.

His kindness was so bright and warm. He told me that there are moments in life when times are just tough for people, and he recognizes his position in being able to offer a helping hand to not only the homeless, but also to single mothers struggling to make ends meet and anyone who happens to be down on their luck. It's more than a comforting, hot meal... it's transcending our tendencies of isolation, it's community, and it's acknowledging the dignity of all walks of life; it's humanity.

He came to the United States with $3. When he was in the works of opening his restaurant with the mission of feeding the homeless, he was met with a lot of backlash. How could he sustain a business with this kind of business model? The people around him were, understandably so, projecting their financial concerns. The beauty is that he recognized the negativity for what it was— fear. The greatest growth happens right on the other side of fear. He was able to set aside that fear only by operating from his heart space. He felt this to be a way for him to align service and success. And he was not wrong. Even though he felt secure in his vision, he met the skeptics with, "Well, even if business fails, I'm pretty sure I will still have more than $3."

The lessons through his light have been the push I need when the bridge did not seem worth crossing— recognize fear as the bridge to greatness, and when something feels right in the heart, let go of the need for society's approval.

When your soul is yearning to be fed, the Universe will undoubtedly provide. You are the creator of your destiny, but first you have to believe it. Envision what you want. Envision what you're doing. See it. Feel it. Believe it. Manifest it. Create it. You will be tested, but we all know the purpose of tests are to improve us. Vibrate in alignment. And it's yours.

THE GREAT MYTH

"Until you make the unconscious conscious, it will direct your life and you will call it fate."

C.G. Jung

From time to time I'll come across knock off motivational quotes that say something along the lines of, "if a girl continues to hold it down for you after you've continuously betrayed her, don't let her go." ICK. What kind of backwards adoration is that? It's a venomous, bitter message disguised as glorifying a woman's strength. The gold medal for being a good partner does not have to be earned through repeated suffering. We have got to end this narrative that a woman's role in a relationship is to rebuild a broken partner. Relationships are meant to ride the waves *together*. Support is not synonymous with savior. When a partner has to play the role of punching bag or therapist, it's no longer a partnership. It's toxic codependency. Relationships aren't always a walk through the park, but the alternative does not have to be trudging through a constant storm. The moment we stop being the target of the wrath *and* the calm after the storm is the moment we send a message to the collective. We are not the fire and the water. We are not flattered by how many times we get back up after being trampled on. We're empowered through peace and growth. We're no longer viewing struggle as the baseline for lasting relationships. Ladies, it really is time that we redefine our tolerance in order to ensure it's congruent with our heart's glow. Going forth, we're not glorifying how many battles we've overcome, we're glorifying leaving anyone who takes us through those battles and keeps us in the shadows.

    We get a similar message when it comes to life. Our belief system has been infiltrated with framing life as an uphill battle, and failure as an inevitable part of it. I disagree. Life doesn't *have* to be hard. If we consider ourselves to be one with nature, it should be easy to digest how things divinely flow with ease and purpose. We admire our deep blue oceans, the heights of our mountains, the breathtaking creatures and flora, the sun that manages to heat an entire planet, and even the galaxies beyond our reach for goodness sake! We're being hurled through space and haven't plopped out of orbit, but we can't fathom the ability to be one with our inner groove and let it guide us through our own little universe? It's so important to understand our own alignment in order to operate with ease. Some way and somehow, nature just works. Do we get the occasional natural disaster and storms? Duh. Ebbs and flows, people. Life gets hard when we resist the current. If we perceive it in a manner that tells us it's meant to be difficult, then we act accordingly and start pushing against the grain because we're "supposed" to. We live once, for a speck of time in the grand scheme of the Universe, yet we believe our time is best spent magnifying the challenges. I'm tired just writing that. Shitty things happen. Point blank. We're emotional beings so we really do feel sad, hurt, angry, worried, and so forth. We should allow ourselves to feel organically, but we shouldn't allow our emotions to rule us. One of the best ways to regulate the emotions is to come back to the present. Just let the emotion *be* without projecting it onto all other areas of life. Just as the storm comes and passes, our emotions can do the same if we allow them to without trapping them, or mentally storing them as content in the "life is hard" category.

A lot of the work involved in making life more enjoyable has to do with reframing perspectives. The most profound reprogramming for me has been around failure. They say that we have to fail before we succeed, and that growth doesn't happen without failure. I really do believe that our best lessons come from the experiences that knock us off track. However, the term "failure" carries a looming cloud of inadequacy. To me, failure is more of a sign to give up rather than continue on. But if failure is again glorified as the precursor to success, is it possible to shift the perspective to be more encouraging than daunting? It goes back to redirection. A failed attempt at weight loss or starting a business is really just the Universe redirecting us to the path of the soul, or the path of the beam. If the conditions are not right for our desired goal to flourish in, the Universe isn't saying no, just not yet. When something we really want falls through, we have a choice to label ourselves as failures and let it seep into the subconscious to serve as a block for any future ideas we try to bring to life. Or we can choose to re-center ourselves and regroup. The saying "go with the flow" doesn't just apply to going along with boring plans your friends make. It's also referring to staying in the flow of Universal order. "Failure" is a form of protection against what was never meant to be ours in the first place. So, the next time you don't quite achieve the reality you desired for yourself, take that time to have a meeting with your inner being and ask for guidance where necessary. Failing doesn't always have to be a sign to reel it back in, it might even be that you're playing too small and are capable of so much more— but perhaps just not yet.

WHY THE HELL NOT?

"Live and let live."

    We're living in a really weird time. Wages have not increased, but housing expenses have, and millennials are forced into overpriced rent and basic living expenses. We're statistically more educated, and simultaneously under paid and in more debt. But I have to say that I have been noticing a shift. My parents' generation lived to work. Financial stability and supporting the family were really the only motivators for working. They worked and continue to work jobs that they don't necessarily enjoy, but "it's a job." There's been a collective shift moving away from that. We want to do work that we actually *enjoy;* that we have a calling to do. But then money and fear prance in, and we sometimes just settle for the conventional route.

    You've seen how my view of an ideal life took some drastic turns. In past generations, veering off course just wasn't even seen as an option, or it was highly frowned upon. Unconventionality somehow became synonymous with below par. If being true to yourself is unconventional, then who wants to be right?! It really is time to cut the ties and honor ourselves authentically, rather than contorting ourselves into a societal mold. It's a luxury that was not afforded to generations before us.

I tell people all the time to create their own personal curriculum. Higher education is at its heights, causing a societal stigma against those who may choose a different route. Finding a job unrelated to one's degree may bring about feelings of wasted time or feeling less than for not working in your field of study. Well, guess what? All of the above are perfectly fine options. Education is invaluable, but we have done it a tremendous disservice by viewing education as the vehicle for obtaining a job. Is education only valued when its tied to work? The role of education should not be solely related to job acquisition. Education, in any form, is a means of mind expansion, exposure to different cultures and time periods in history. Learning is good for our brains! But education has also served as a hindrance. From my own experience of totally not working in the field I majored in, one can feel like she is at a loss if her dreams and desires have evolved into something else.

I think the first step is to appreciate education for what it is— mastering skill sets and broadening our scope about the world we live in. But if we unpack our inner pulls and realize we want to explore different routes, then I only have one question, why the hell not?! It's perfectly okay to keep learning new things. Whether it's through self-study, certification courses, or going back to school with a different focus. Being educated cannot and should not be capped, and it definitely should not only be considered valid if it's from a formal institution.

I had a student who was a renowned scientist, but was toppling with the idea of becoming a professor. He had always felt connected to mentorship. He had some concerns, though. He knew his family, and probably anyone else in his circle, would be disappointed that he'd leave his highly regarded position to be a professor. I told him that he is the only one who knows his connection best and the only one who can honor it. I love this example because it's a testament to how even in the most prominent situations, if one does not feel aligned, not even an elite status can trump the heart's desire. If you're no longer radiating from the inside out, it's not only a disservice to yourself, but to the collective field.

In a perfect world, everyone would feel empowered to keep adding to their personal curriculum. We would be able to more easily allow ourselves to take the unconventional path because we would know that unconventionality is often times the uncovering of authenticity. Beyond study and work, we would do as we please without first considering societal opinion or judgment. Why not start that blog? Or go to karaoke on a Tuesday? The point is to just be and do. We are completely consumed with how things should be, how we should dress, how we should work, and every other should phrase ingrained in our brain. It's time to stop comparing and start creating. Because again, why not?

KNOW YOUR LINE

"You can, you should, and if you're brave enough to start, you will."

Stephen King

Before I left for that infamous trip to Greece, my grandma begged me not to go. She was convinced that the trip would be riddled with danger. I always knew that she wasn't keen on international travel unless it was back to Sicily, but I really didn't understand where this deep, dark fear was coming from. It was sort of funny to me in an "Oh, Nonna is just worried about me" kind of way. As we all know, I didn't honor her request. If going to Greece with friends for a week rattled her, how do you think she took the whole moving to Rome thing? I don't have to answer that. My mom's view on adventure is not far off from my grandma's— "but is it safe??" She was married young, and very driven by career and family. Adventure and leisurely travel didn't quite fit in with the program, nor was it highly sought after.

After moving and taking my own leaps, people would say, "oh wow you're brave." I guess? I knew it was out of the ordinary, especially in my family, but was there actually a disconnect between me and the line of women before me?

I'll start with my sister. I don't know how she does it, but she is the most grounded and level-headed person ever. If there's a crisis, you want her in your corner. I'd go to her with "life-threatening" injuries and anxieties, and she'd be able to grapple the situation effortlessly. One time my cat's paw was stuck under the refrigerator and I was running around panicking ready to call the fire department. She remained calm to balance my crazy, and voilà, the cat's paw broke free. She definitely made fun of me after (and still does) but you get the picture. Maybe the big sister role had a lot to do with it, but she has had such a striking independence for as long as I can remember. It carried with her through nursing school, becoming a wife and mother, and being the go-to for nurturing and guidance. She has the magic potion when it comes to just figuring things out. The admiration is endless, and to me, this kind of independence and self-reliance is beyond brave.

My mom is my number two critic (number one being myself), but she moves heaven and earth to support and provide. I'd never tell her this, but at times I just feel so unworthy. (Hi, mom, if you're reading this). Safety and comfort are her driving forces, but she somehow manages to dig deep to validate my unconventional approach to life. When we were little, she worked full time, would pick us up after school, take us home to change, start dinner, drive us to practice, and make it back home to have dinner on the table by the time my dad got home from work. I definitely thought that's just what moms did. Which is true for some family dynamics, but it wasn't until I got older that I was able to truly grasp the significance of balancing motherhood and career. She was in constant mama mode. As someone who needs alone time to recharge, looking back on how packed each moment of the day was for her provokes a suffocating feeling in me. But she always showed up! Her whys were definitely stronger than her hows. That's a live action super woman right there.

Remembering my dad's mom reminds me a lot of my sister. She always had such a calming energy. She lived in Sicily so I didn't see her often, but I'm not sure I ever saw her get riled up about anything. In her early years of marriage, she moved back and forth from Sicily to Argentina where my grandfather found work. They had small children at the time, and moving from continent to continent then was not nearly as feasible as it is now. They had five children, didn't have much money, the siblings had to share beds, and yet, my dad still has happy stories to tell. He always remembers the homemade pasta she'd make every Sunday. Life in Sicily with lack of work and five children was tough. But still, they provided. Her motherly touch is the imprint left on their hearts, not so much the fact that they had to cut the front of their shoes when they began to grow out of them.

My mom's mom, the fiery grandma who didn't want me to go on vacation, has a special place in my heart. I am her name sake, and I spent a lot of time with her when I was little during my days of struggling with going to school. We cooked together and made sure to always be done in the kitchen by the time Oprah and Judge Judy came on. We always say her hands, in all essence of the word, have the magic touch. She can design and sew any type of clothing or gown, provide the alterations on your prom dress, and in the kitchen, she could probably make a feast out of scraps. We honor her as the matriarch, and deservingly so. I never viewed her much as a risk taker, but that didn't diminish her spark any less. During a course in the process of my holistic healing and coaching certification, the class practiced a regression technique. To be honest, I didn't really get it and may have even been a skeptic. For any non "woo-woo" people reading this, just stick with me. It was my turn to be the client while another student practiced the technique as the practitioner. We were focusing on positive regression, meaning I chose something that I wanted to manifest in the hopes of discovering resources from my past to provide guidance. I decided to manifest speaking events to empower women and girls, something I had a growing passion for. We started the process, and immediately, things got interesting. I mentally landed at a shipyard dock. Standing in front of me was my grandma at a much younger age. I recognized her because I had seen a picture of her at that age before. She was standing there with a toddler on her hip. She was looking at me with a soft smile, but said nothing at all. I knew. This inexplicable knowing washed over me. The message penetrated the depths of my soul. She had come to the United States by boat in 1961 at the age of 21 by herself with a baby to meet my grandfather who had already come to the States prior. Eight days and 10 nights at sea. She was the representation of woman- empowerment that I wanted to draw out of the women I speak to. She has never been the type to voice self-empowerment or strength, but that generational energy transcended her outwardly reserved persona. She was a symbol of empowerment in the flesh, validation that I have it in me to share with other women, and inspiration to follow through with *my* version of living my dream life.

It was then that I really honed in on this line of bravery and strength that I come from, that I'm surrounded by. This will to be the driver of life may have manifested differently for my grandmothers, my mom, my sister, and me, but the roots were so firmly planted and can sustain such a vast array of fruits. Considering our generational foundation while we're in the midst of building our own legacies can be the impetus we need to not only live well for ourselves, but also for the next. Sometimes, generational cycles should be broken, but in this case, I'd like to see the line evolve and continue.

FLUID WELLNESS

"We need to do a better job of putting ourselves higher on our own 'to do' list."

Michelle Obama

Everyone has their own idea of wellness. Self-care and wellness weren't really discussed in my house, and they definitely were not a priority. I thought of wellness as sort of a treat when time allowed. A warm bath, going for a pedicure, relaxing by the pool. It was sort of an escape from being on the go with the day to day responsibilities.

The only good thing about my 9-5 job was the commute (aside from the overwhelming impending dread). My creative drive was on fire. I was so motivated to do writing projects and figure out the appropriate next steps for a career change. I'd somehow get through the dreadful day, go to the gym, and by the time I got home I was depleted. All of the excitement and spark I had in the morning had completely vanished. Even when I did have down time, my energy just wasn't right. I felt myself going in a downward spiral. This was my first taste of compartmentalizing my energy and wellness. My creativity being stifled in an unfulfilling environment transmuted into me being unhappy with every other part of my life. The dark matter left the office with me and permeated my spirit. Even though I began the day with such conviction, in that state of bliss from thinking about the things I felt most connected to, it wasn't enough to come out of the other side of the work day on top. As a result, depression was on the horizon. Trapping the heartfelt energy was so damaging to my holistic health. I really did think it was possible to somehow be miserable for 8 hours a day and snap back into feeling whole when I got home. All I was doing was separating surviving and thriving, and let me tell you, it did not work. If going to work sucks the joy out of everything else you love, it's time to consider if sacrificing the essence of who you for a job is really worth it or not.

After being back home from Rome for a few months, the teaching job wasn't drowning my soul like that awful 9-5, but it wasn't exactly lighting it up, either. While I was in the pre-launch stages of getting my business together, a really profound shift in me happened. The stark divide between working and incorporating self-care became really enhanced and emphasized. The duality of doing life and life doing me honestly felt like a rip off. I started to really hone in on this deep knowing of wellness being fluid, where work and responsibilities are an extension of living well. The thought of coming home after work being a saving grace from the day really didn't sit well with me. Why do we compartmentalize wellness? I sat with the feeling and explored exactly what it was I was seeking. I needed to be working part-time while working on my business, but did it have to be something I didn't feel very connected to? I wanted to go to work and be surrounded by like-hearted people in an energetically healthy atmosphere. That way, when I came home, I wouldn't be running for the door in desperation for peace, but I'd now have the energy to actually work on my projects.

    I decided to take some action and started working at a wellness center. The craziest thing was that their mission aligned perfectly with my new understanding of what it means to be well. Work and wellness do not have to be opposites, but rather can co-exist. I was able to put more work into my book and my business on my days off because my energy had not been sucked dry in an environment not suited for me. Part of me answering to the calling of holistic coaching was honoring wellness as a lifestyle; I just didn't quite know that's what I was doing until further down the road. It dawned on me that not being physically or mentally ill did not at all mean that we knew how to live well. The days of going to work and being miserable were over. Of course, being at work comes with a certain amount of stress and challenges, but it does not have to only serve as a means to a financial end. Think of the compartments of life as subjects in school. You could excel tremendously in language and arts, and completely bomb math and science. In that case, your GPA is probably around a mediocre C. (I understand that a GPA isn't the ultimate measure of intelligence and C's are perfectly fine. It's just an example— don't chop off my head.) When we parcel out wellness, we end up with an overall mediocre or even miserable lifestyle. If wellness doesn't permeate cumulatively, it makes it difficult to be at our best even in the parts of life that we do enjoy. Much like one would need a tutor for the difficult subjects in school, sometimes it's necessary to consult with a professional in order to address and clear the blockages that hold us back from doing what it takes to live well. Old patterns, beliefs, and programming linger in the subconscious and can actually be the reason we feel stagnant or stuck. Being mentally and emotionally drained from work doesn't leave you full enough to be as present and connected at home, in relationships, etc. To me, wellness must flow. It means to not only stay well health wise, but to also take care of our energy. Some of us have to align ourselves in purpose and service when it comes to jobs and careers. We owe it to ourselves and to those affected by our work. Work well in order to come home and live well.

I can't end this chapter without addressing the opposite scenario— work being a relief from home life. I've seen countless examples of people who stay at work late because it beats out going home to a toxic relationship. This one really sent a spear through the heart. Home and love are supposed to be our sanctuaries, not our prisons. We have to be better at honoring our hearts. We have to know that we are deserving of a well-rounded, wholesome life. Neglecting our needs can really lead us down a variety of avenues of self-destruction. Individually and collectively, we are worth far beyond the traps we fall into. I can't wait for the day when we have a collective understanding that living well has to be a priority, not a privilege.

THIS IS WHY

"The moment you doubt whether you can fly, you cease forever to be able to do it."

J.M. Barrie

I was walking through D.C. one day when I came across a "this is why" person. A mother and daughter had been on a stroll when bird droppings landed right on the girl's shoulder. She screamed, and then laughed, and luckily her mom had a tissue with her to clean up the mess. As she wiped her shoulder, the mom said, "This is why I always carry around a pack of Kleenex." Is that really why? To be on guard for bird poop? Or is it for a more practical reason such as a runny nose? Now, yes this is lighthearted and harmless, but how often do we grunt "this is why" after something unfortunate happens?

For example, someone who reads a story about a celebrity cheating scandal may say something like, "This is why I don't trust men." Another person who didn't get hired may say, "This is why I don't even bother with trying anymore." "This is why…" is a defense mechanism used to take one bad thing and generalize it across the board as to why we should refrain from ever doing anything ever again. "This is why men don't like me." "This is why I can never catch a break." The words we say to ourselves enter our belief system. Even if it's just in the heat of the moment, we don't recognize the damage of constantly making these deprecating, general statements. It doesn't help to take on some level of blame every time things go wrong. I do this a lot! We say it as if we already knew how something would turn out. We didn't know. We're just upset and end up internalizing. But, interestingly, when things go right, we don't generalize how good we have it, rather regard it as an isolated event and attribute it to happenstance or luck.

We have to be careful about saying things like this to other people, too. Words have power, and while they vanish from our tongues in seconds, they can last indefinitely on the ears they fall on. Offering advice or constructive criticism is a lot different than pinning blame with a connotation of inferiority. Saying, "This is why you shouldn't be using dating apps" after someone gets stood up is helping how, exactly? We need to be mindful of what we say and how we say it. These are real life instances where the intention may be right, but the application is not. Our brains are sponges and information involuntarily gets stored. *This* is why we have to be selective and intentional with how we speak to ourselves and to others. We have to make it a daily practice to avoid the self-created dark cloud, because as we know, what we believe is what we attract. No one wants to be the "this is why" bird poop hero.

REVERSE WEBMD

"Don't be a victim of negative self-talk— remember YOU are listening."

Bob Proctor

When we're sick or discover something unusual on ourselves, the first logical step would be to go see a doctor. Instead, we tend to enter into the black hole vortex that is the internet. Chronic illnesses, rare diseases, you name it, we've all diagnosed ourselves at some point. We somehow manage to match our symptoms to the most extreme illness and actually *believe* we may have it. Internet diagnostics can be frightening! It hit me one day how we follow this exact pattern of pending doom in non-medical scenarios.

We can be surrounded by loving and uplifting people 99% of the time, but somehow that one negative interaction with someone barrels its way to the forefront of our attention. We obsess over it, internalize it, and even generalize that interaction to convince ourselves that this must be everyone else's opinion, too. Our tendency to hold the negatives on a pedestal is the reason we find it easier to bond over trauma rather than triumph; the reason we can date good people but still be completely consumed with the guy who treated us terribly. Focusing on the worst-case scenario is easier, it's safer. We give so much weight to mean comments, not getting hired, or not being included for a couple of reasons. First, any of these things that hurt us is penetrating our ego. The ego becomes defensive; it has an image to uphold! Secondly, the role of the subconscious mind is to protect us. These negative experiences tap on any and everything that has negatively impacted us in the past and ignites this fire in us to focus on the danger for our safety purposes. We needed this function during the hunting and gathering times in order to measure a survival risk, but we don't need to rely on it nearly as much today. Especially not for social interactions.

We do this thing where we are afraid to get excited about the things we want because we feel that thinking the worst will leave us less disappointed if what we want doesn't happen. As if expecting the worst will take the sting off if the worst manifests instead. Preparing for the worst lowers our frequency and vibration. Focus on radiating the energy you want to attract! I understand not wanting to shout from the rooftops about the dream job we applied to. I am a firm believer that negative energy from other people can impact us. But why not personally lean into the experience fully? There's a difference between preserving and being selective about the energy surrounding what we want, and self-sabotaging through feeding our subconscious mind with the expectation of failure. Cheating ourselves of joy in the moment makes life way more of a drab than it needs to be. It's perfectly okay to get excited, and it's also okay if things don't always unfold in our favor. The key in relieving the sting isn't to hide behind a wall of low expectation, but instead to trust. You have to trust with every fiber of your being in the power of Universal intelligence. We may not get what we want, and while it does hurt, we have to have this unwavering faith that what is meant for our highest good will not pass us. I mentioned before how it's easier to keep a tight grip on the bad things that did happen and that could happen. It keeps us boxed. When we're intimidated or hurt, we protect ourselves by keeping within those bounds. No action or risk has to be taken in the box of victimhood. We simply convince ourselves that we aren't worth playing big so we retreat. Why even bother if I'm not good enough? It's easier than being vulnerable or susceptible to getting hurt again or failing to achieve certain goals for ourselves. But how limiting of a life is this? We can't control how others perceive us or treat us, but the real damage is when we internalize and turn on the negative self-talk. That self-talk is again the subconscious bubbling to the surface, and is exactly like the internet vortex— vast and potentially damaging.

    We typically don't start on the motivational internet sources, but instead on the more intense ones that tell us how bad off we are. What if when it comes to our negative experiences and the way we talk to ourselves, we flip the script, a kind of reverse WebMD, where we focus on the other side of what if. What if it goes right? What if what that person said to me is a reflection of them and not me? What if I feel safe in getting excited rather than staying guarded and preparing for the worst? On the other side of what if is a raised vibration, an energy field that you *want* to be matched. Get vulnerable and get excited because what if everything you've ever wanted also wants you?

LONELY VERSUS ALONE

"You cannot be lonely if you like the person you're alone with."

Wayne Dyer

I am someone who absolutely needs to be alone to recharge. Being around too many people and too much energy drains me. For a while I would give a bug-eyed, cocked-head look at people who refueled off of other people— half in judgment and half in confusion. It sounded like a nightmare to me, but it also met my ears with a tone of dependency. How the hell is alone time the enemy? The reason that I casted judgment on those people is because of my own experience with alone time. Before understanding and mastering the tools of restoring my own energy, I was those people! Alone time felt uneasy. I needed to be doing something or with someone. A Friday night home doing nothing was unheard of. My alone time was so intimidating because I was alone with my thoughts and anxieties that I really had no idea how to manage. I needed an outlet to distract me. Again, all glory given to Rome, having to go through certain things alone forced me to put in the energy work. I had to heal and put the pieces back together by myself. Now, I cannot imagine using my previous coping and recharging mechanisms. They are so foreign to me. I fully recognize why I projected judgment on the ones who aren't fond of alone time as being dependent because *I was dependent.* That revelation also shed some light on a few other reasons for why and when we judge people. Judgment is the product of projecting our own negative perceptions on to other people as their reality, and projecting our own insecurities when people do something outside of our comfort zone.

I fully understand that not everyone operates the same way. I am aware that introverts and extroverts meet their needs differently. It is not that one is mightier than the other, it is just the way in which we honor our unique wiring. I do, however, urge you to get uncomfortable for a moment. If you recharge from being around people, is it an escape mechanism or a genuine fill from surrounding energy? The former is an extremely self-limiting approach to growth. It hinders self-reflection, self-love, inner healing, and strengthening the God given tools we have to replenish ourselves. It sucks to sit there with our thoughts and emotions. Our mind can take us down unforeseen paths and convince us that we're stuck in that place until we decide to run away from ourselves in order to seek validation or to dilute our energy with the energy of others. It's okay to feel uneasy! Be gentle and take it as an opportunity to get in touch with yourself. Humans are biologically meant to travel in packs, I totally get it. But emotional dependency and lack of self-growth is harmful to the collective. Remember, we're only as strong as the weakest link.

As much as I am for having the confidence to trust in our aloneness, I am equally for finding a tribe. Who you surround yourself with is important. Whether it's family or friends, be selective and exclusive when it comes to who you share such intimate space with. Not everyone is for you, but more importantly, not everyone is good for you. Build a tribe rooted in love, honesty, support, and growth. Your tribe should want to see you win, should root for you, and should help you up when you lose. Some people are lucky enough to have the same core, long term friends. But as humans who grow and evolve; many of us shed some skin along the way. I think one of the biggest misconceptions people have when it comes to friends diverging down different paths is that there's this big, dark cloud over that connection and disconnection. Outgrowing doesn't equate to enemies. You can allow the outgrown friendships to roam and still wish each other well. Your tribe should be the product of a gravitational pull, rather than an artificial force.

In loving ourselves dynamically, we can feel just as safe and empowered in solitude as we do when surrounded by our people.

CUSTOM MADE

"You are the only you there is and ever will be."

Jen Sincero

I had a bit of an epiphany one day while I was driving. I was listening to an episode of Oprah's Super Soul Sunday podcast and during an interview, Oprah had mentioned how truly divine her creation was from the point of conception. She shared how she was conceived after her parents had been intimately involved only one time. *Oprah! One time!* If that doesn't serve as a symbolic illustration for how extraordinary and full of purpose we all are, then I'm not sure what does.

There is no other being in existence that is just like you or me in mind, body, and spirit. Really considering how uniquely crafted we are from our cellular level constructs all the way to our consciousness is major! It's as if each of us is a custom-made, one of a kind model— human edition. You are mystical. Out of all the DNA combinations possible, the Universal conditions led to the perfectly unique creation of *you*.

Since we have such infinite value just from existing, we should feel divinely supported in being ultra-selective about who allow to share our intimate space with. Picture this and lean fully into it. You are a custom-made Ferrari. Every detail has been carefully and intentionally crafted. There are other Ferraris on the planet, but none of them are made or operate like you. If you are the driver of this original, priceless machine, then a significant other is the passenger. You drive through life authentically, going where you want when you want. Your mind and heart are the keys, the force that affords you the ability to move through life as you intend. Along the way, you pick up some passengers. You've invited this passenger in to enjoy the ride with you. You have standards for how passengers should comport themselves during the ride. You probably want a passenger who talks to you, listens to you, supports you, laughs with you, and helps with directions from time to time. As the driver, you have the sole power to decide if you feel as if the passenger is pleasant to have alongside you, or if the passenger should be dismissed for disrespecting and devaluing the Ferrari by leaving a mess, being careless, or failing to appreciate the spirit of your divinely crafted being. You can either tolerate the diminishment of your worth, or pull over to gracefully let them out. Keeping in mind how masterful your creation is, it's still your choice. You may even start to hand over the keys. In which case, you would be losing the essence of your intended path by allowing someone else to be the driver. Luckily, you can take the keys back at any moment. You may very well find yourself as the passenger in someone else's custom-made creation. What kind of passenger are you? Do you try to be the driver?

I think by now you get the picture. The moment we have a passenger who tarnishes our sacred being, we have to ask ourselves how much we actually value ourselves. Are we protecting our worth? The ride may get bumpy. But for it to be enjoyable, the driver must feel safe in leading with authenticity while also feeling connected to and supported by the passenger. Journeying in union flows most efficiently when the driver and the passenger respectively honor their roles. Don't be afraid to (literally and figuratively) kick someone to the curb! If you don't set the standard and be the gate keeper, the passenger can easily become a heavy burden. And, honestly, who wants to be cruising down the highway of life, sun shining and wind blowing, with someone who views or treats you as a raggedy old go-kart?

HOLISTIC HARMONY

"Wellness encompasses a healthy body, a sound mind, and a tranquil spirit. Enjoy the journey as you strive for wellness."

Laurette Gagnon Beaulieu

Do you know yourself holistically? The interconnectedness of your mind, body and spirit? In high school, I suffered with severe stomach issues that doctors couldn't really find a diagnosis for. All tests and procedures came back clear, but I was physically ill. One doctor finally told me that it was due to stress. I felt the fire igniting in me. I'm sick all of the time and you want to boil it down to some stupid, irrelevant stress?? I knew my body. I knew that certain foods were triggering. What I didn't know was that he was right. Stress, tension, and mismanaged energy really did impact my physical health. Just as certain foods I ate impacted my energy and mental health. I actually didn't know myself, my holistic self, as well as I thought I did. The system makes perfect sense when we consider how intertwined our mind, body, and spirit are. It's why we get that nauseating feeling after heartbreak or trauma, and why being deficient in certain nutrients disrupts our mental and emotional health.

If you've ever followed someone's weight loss or fitness journey, you may have noticed the total shift in mindset that accompanied the physical transformations. It's a testament to how imperative it is for our mind, body, and spirit to be in accordance as we transcend to our optimal state of being. On the same token, the holistic alignment can be seen amongst the highly in-tune spiritual beings of the world. It is common that the deeper someone delves into their spirituality and the higher their consciousness becomes, mindful eating develops as a lifestyle practice. Considering not only the kind of foods they eat, but also the energy used in producing the food is seen as having a direct impact on one's own energetic well-being. I understand that this comprehensive inclusivity is not a common awareness. I know that we all function from the heights of our own awareness, but taking time to explore ourselves holistically can really shed some light on how significant the internal and external aspects of our lives impact our overall health.

Having our holistic selves in alignment is optimal. Any imbalances can manifest in various ways which is why self-awareness is key in overall health. Part of knowing ourselves fully is knowing when we need to seek professional help or other resources. As much as I promote self-empowerment, self-empowerment very much is recognizing when help is needed and acting on it. It's self-care in its most basic form. There are physicians, practitioners, and healers out there who have devoted their energy to bringing forth wellness in others. Their gifts are meant to be shared. We don't need to have all of the answers when it comes to transforming our health, but we should recognize the power in asking the questions. When we don't feel well, or perpetually feel "off", it's our responsibility to prioritize our wellness in discovering how our biological and spiritual needs should be met. Our body serves as a great messenger. Listen to it and nurture it. It not only represents our physical embodiment, but it houses our spirit. Looking good *and* feeling good come with the territory of living in holistic harmony, which should always be on the agenda.

YOUNIVERSE

"'Cause I'm a woman
Phenomenally.
Phenomenal woman,
That's me."

Maya Angelou

  I did not know that spiritual growth would have such a profound effect on my connectedness to the Universe. I began the journey looking for answers on how to sort through emotional wrecks. It beautifully unraveled in ways I could have never imagined. My patterns of thinking and processing have been reconditioned, more aligned with my highest good. I learned that every push-back came with an even stronger push-forward. Trusting and surrendering to the power of the Universe is the way to creating the lives we were meant to live. I learned that it is faith that carries us closer to the beam, not hope. And I realized that self-discovery is infinite.

We can succumb to our experiences, or we can view the experiences as a flashlight; a flashlight on all of the inner work hiding under the shadows needing to be done. We can make a conscious choice that our past will not be a foreshadowing of our future. We have no responsibility or control over past situations, but we do have control of rerouting the patterns. We have more of a say in our destiny than we are made to believe. Each and every one of us is worthy of enjoying life. When worthiness gets cloudy, it's our job to step into our magic and clear the fog.

As the world rotates in unison, it provides a perspective of connectedness. As far and wide as this Universe goes, it is also quite small. Humans from all walks of life have shared experiences, and that energy binds us tightly together. While it may be a small world after all, the Universe is infinite in possibility and abundance. When we tap into this duality of our likeness with each other and with nature, and with the vastness of the Universe beyond our scope, we truly become one. Being one with the Universe is realizing that the Universe flows not only around us, but through us. The Universal energy is there to guide and protect us, but only if the gates are open; only if we *allow* ourselves to be receptive of the divine energy. This is how we embark on the never-ending journey of self-discovery. As the Universe is ever-flowing, so is our growth and expansion in consciousness. Revel on the magic carpet ride of life.

Before you take another step out into the real world,

venture into the Youniverse. The treasures within are worth discovering, polishing, and sharing with the world. Remember that you are nothing short of majestic and intentionally crafted. There is no one else on this earth who can outshine your worth or your purpose. You are the *only* you. Love, protect, and nurture the phenomenon that you are. Breathe in the energy of the Universe, allow it to gently direct you. The magical life you want is awaiting you because you are divinely crowned and supported. Step over the blocks and power through the noise. Feel your way forward, and know that you have permission to follow the beam. We are all rooting for you because when you win, we all win. So, from the warmest depths of my heart: When the Universe speaks, listen; because listening to the Universe is listening to yourself.

Thank you to the creatives who made it all possible:

Cover Shot by KarenTang Photography

Book Cover Designed by Claire Luigard

Hair/Makeup/Body Art by Olivia Sahadeo, Nicole Lambert, Santina De Luca

Editing by Monica Potts

Holistic Healing and Coaching services:

Healing and Empowerment Resolutions, LLC

healingempower.com

Stressors: _____

_____

_____

_____

_____

Gratitude: _____

_____

_____

_____

_____

Goals: _____

_____

_____

_____

_____

Stressors: _____

_____

_____

_____

_____

Gratitude: _____

_____

_____

_____

_____

Goals: _____

_____

_____

_____

_____

Stressors: _____

_____

_____

_____

_____

Gratitude: _____

_____

_____

_____

_____

Goals: _____

_____

_____

_____

_____

Stressors: _____

_____

_____

_____

_____

Gratitude: _____

_____

_____

_____

_____

Goals: _____

_____

_____

_____

_____

Stressors: _____

_____

_____

_____

_____

Gratitude: _____

_____

_____

_____

_____

Goals: _____

_____

_____

_____

_____

Stressors: _____

_____

_____

_____

_____

Gratitude: _____

_____

_____

_____

_____

Goals: _____

_____

_____

_____

_____

Stressors: _____

_____

_____

_____

_____

Gratitude: _____

_____

_____

_____

_____

Goals: _____

_____

_____

_____

_____

Stressors: _____

_____

_____

_____

_____

Gratitude: _____

_____

_____

_____

_____

Goals: _____

_____

_____

_____

_____

Stressors: _____

_____

_____

_____

_____

Gratitude: _____

_____

_____

_____

_____

Goals: _____

_____

_____

_____

_____

Stressors: _____

_____

_____

_____

_____

Gratitude: _____

_____

_____

_____

_____

Goals: _____

_____

_____

_____

_____

Stressors: _____

_____

_____

_____

_____

Gratitude: _____

_____

_____

_____

_____

Goals: _____

_____

_____

_____

_____

Made in the USA
Middletown, DE
16 February 2020